WESSEX MEM

Country Essays

by

Llewelyn Powys

Edited with an Introduction
by Peter J. Foss

THE
POWYS
PRESS

2003

THE POWYS PRESS
is an imprint of The Powys Society,
82 Linden Road, Gloucester GL1 5HD

© 2003
Sally Connely and the Estate of Llewelyn Powys
*Introduction, Notes and non-photographic
illustrations*: Peter J. Foss
Typographical arrangement: Stephen Powys Marks

ISBN 1 874559 27 9

This publication has been set in
Bitstream Arrus and Century Old Style
in PageMaker 6.5 on a Macintosh Computer

Cover: ***View towards Portland from Dungy Head,***
detail from a painting in oils by Peter J. Foss, 1994.
Back cover: ***Llewelyn Powys in New York,*** *photograph by
Doris Ulmann, 1928 (by courtesy of Stephen Powys Marks)*

Printed by Anthony Williams, printer (tel: 0117 986 0431)

Contents

Introduction

Llewelyn Powys was that intriguing literary hybrid—a freelance journalist who was also a 'man of letters'. For many years in the 1920s Powys made a small living out of his journalism—the incidents and experiences, mostly of his days in Africa, which he contributed to the pages of the *New York Evening Post*, together with stories and biographical portraits to the *Freeman*, the *Mentor* and the *Dial*. His numerous book reviews and short notices which appeared from 1920 to 1924, show how far he had trained himself to summarise a book, to express an intelligent opinion, turn a phrase and hold the reader's attention for what he wanted to say as well as what the book tells us. And he was to pursue this journalistic skill into the 1930s, after his return to England in 1925, in articles submitted both to local newspapers such as the *Dorset Daily Echo* and to national broadsheets such as the *Daily Herald*, where he was much valued. The abundance of this kind of work in contributions to newspapers and magazines awaits bibliographical referencing (in progress), but the essays and reviews probably amount to near a thousand.

The other side of this coin is the distinction here drawn between the journalist and the literary man. Llewelyn Powys believed profoundly in the value and importance of literature as an expression of the individual imagination. In witness to this conviction his distinctive style, whilst on occasions leaning towards artifice, was always revealing of a mind that was eager and idiosyncratic, and always in a creative way engaged with the object of his interest. This is clearly evident in the style of the pieces that follow which all date from the 1930s when Powys's writing had developed a rich patina of rhetorical and verbal dexterity which his wife Alyse Gregory once likened to branches overburdened with their fruit. Nonetheless there was a method in the artifice, for it not only recalled the style of Powys's admired seventeenth century authors, but it reproduced something of their hermetical purpose. The parenthetical sentence and the singing line, with its figurative devices, its use of archaisms and hyphenation, and the aphoristic well of allusions upon which it draws, produces the effect of something age-old and hieratic, indeed something that catches at a truth.

Llewelyn Powys was born in 1884 into a Victorian vicarage family, the fifth son of the Revd Charles Francis Powys, vicar of Montacute, Somerset. He was educated in the family tradition at Sherborne School, Dorset, and Corpus Christi College, Cambridge, but he was no scholar and he drifted for a number of years in and out of schoolmastering before the onset of a tubercular condition determined the remainder of his life. From 1909 onwards Powys was dogged by his consumptive disease which at periods rendered him a semi-invalid. So that when he retired to Dorset in 1925, his intention was to pursue his vocation as a writer as best he could for the years left to him, living in accordance with the 'poetic faith' that became a corner-stone of his philosophy, and practising his literary craft in periodicals not only to earn money but also to give expression to his individual imaginative vision. Most of the essays of this period were republished in five collections between 1934 and 1939, beginning with *Earth Memories* (1934) and ending with *A Baker's Dozen*, published just after Powys died in Switzerland in 1939. The latter contained mostly reminiscences of his childhood in Montacute, whilst those essays which dealt with local places and characters in the West Country were collected into *Dorset Essays* (1935) and *Somerset Essays* (1937)—a selection of which was republished, with an Introduction by John Cowper Powys, under the title *Somerset and Dorset Essays* in 1957. The essays in the present book represent a selection of the remainder, most of them published in some form or another, but not previously brought together.

It is not easy to pin-point the particular place Llewelyn Powys holds in our contemporary literature. W. J. Keith, for example, in his book *The Rural Tradition* (1975), discusses Powys in relation to criteria he lays down for a tradition of English rural writing among authors such as Borrow, Cobbett, Jefferies and Hudson. They include characteristics, also present in Powys, such as a concentration on a particular geographical area, knowledge of natural history and a sense of the religious, or at least awe, in the presence of Nature. Keith also

6

distinguishes a style, usually discursive, which excels in the essay format, and among the writers discussed in this context, it is perhaps Richard Jefferies (1848–1887) who comes closest in comparison to Llewelyn Powys's work. In Jefferies a concern for 'essential truth' over literalness, and something of a formlessness in its transmission, is present as it is in Powys. Whilst Richard Jefferies and W. H. Hudson are not identified wholly with a particular geographical area, both brought a shaping imagination to the examination of phenomena, combining natural history with the life of the spirit. This was achieved partly through the operation of memory. As Jefferies wrote, 'it is not only what you actually see along the path, but what you remember to have seen that gives it its beauty.' Interestingly, both these writers recognised the problem of memory's distorting perspective, but both were unapologetic, since merely to observe and analyse was to remain wedded to 'single vision', whereas the exercise of imagination in recollection was, as Wordsworth had shown, to see into the life of things.

'Memory' is very much the key word in Llewelyn Powys's writing, for, as he says, the initial purpose of memory in his own case is to counter the pain of the present and to 'open the door of his mind'. Written against a background of acute illness, many of these essays present an 'I' which adopts the role of *revenant*, re-creating past experience with the vividness of a lantern-slide. But it is also a means of merging the seeing eye and the 'eloquent I' in the individuated poetic vision. As with the essay on the Bronze Age settlement in the lonely valley near his home ('Chainey Bottom') the hidden structures of other worlds might be revealed by combining observation with a kind of racial memory and intuition. Llewelyn Powys's power as a writer, in this respect, was recognised at the time these essays were written, for a reviewer of the American edition of *Earth Memories* (1938), wrote of the 'memory that can relate an ordinary experience of an ordinary day to some primitive impulse or intuitively recalled event of a past age':

> He has felt that entire universes of meaning and emotion are contained in the flutter of a wing or the simplest manifestation of beautiful organic growth.

The present collection rounds off with a group of 'memory' essays evocative of Llewelyn Powys's Montacute background on the borders of Somerset and Dorset. Others intersperse biographical studies—on Hardy, Wordsworth, Fuller and Hudson—with essays about landscape, gypsies, wild life, archaeology and place-names. Here is mostly a Dorset perspective—from the white cliffs of Lulworth and Chaldon, known so well to Llewelyn Powys, to the far west of Broadwindsor and Racedown, from the sea at Chesil to the woods of Sherborne and the Blackmore Vale.

As with other writers of the rural tradition, it is Llewelyn Powys's distinction of attitude, style and personality that makes his writing remarkable, quite apart from what he has to say about the country and its life; and we recognise him as one of that small band of 'dispossessed spiritual seekers' who, with writers such as Henry Williamson and H. J. Massingham, carried on the rural tradition of Jefferies and Hudson into our own time.

Green Corners of Dorset

On one occasion when I was travelling in a crowded New York subway with my brother John I noticed upon his face an expression of extraordinary beatific happiness. As I watched him holding to a strap like an upside-down parrot, surrounded by a crowd of jostling city workers, I wondered what on earth could have got into his foolish head to render him so little incommoded by his inconvenient predicament. Arrived at our destination I ventured to ask him what the thoughts were that had been so pleasing to him. He reminded me of a tombstone that we both knew in the churchyard of the village of Burpham in Sussex. It was a stone that we had often looked at with pleasure. It marked the final resting-place of a shepherd. I have now forgotten the man's name, but the simple inscription had ended with the proud unexpected words 'of Dorset'.

The shepherd had in the early years of Queen Victoria's reign learned his trade in Dorset, perhaps on the Ballard Downs or on the grey-walled uplands around St Ealdhelm's Head, or on some such sheep-run far away in Wessex; and although his bones were now destined to rest for ever amongst those of the South Saxons it seemed that he, or his family, had no mind to allow his earlier associations to be forgotten. My brother went on to explain that, unheedful of the swarming subway throng, he had been imagining himself lying in a grave next to this old shepherd of the farm in a condition of ineffable quiet, of ineffable peace. His words filled me with astonishment. Meditations of the kind he described could never have done me a service. Not at any time of my life have I felt the least envy to be 'free amongst the dead'. Always I would prefer the scurviest sort of existence—that of a rag-and-bone man, of a closet cleaner even—to this cursed future lodging 'where thunder-clap was never heard'.

> The weariest and most loathed worldly life
> That age, ache, penury, and imprisonment
> Can lay on nature is a paradise
> To what we fear of death.

However, the hint I had received of the mind's power of liberating itself I never forgot; and ever since, when I am in company I dislike, or when I am sick, or when I am unduly agitated, it has been my custom to open wide the mind's cage door and let my thoughts escape to certain spots in Dorset, 'green corners' of my native county that I know and love.

Often in my present exile I have returned as a *revenant* to The White Nose. I see the proud promontory in February, when the ravens are beginning to 'theek' their dizzy nests; when the lambs are bleating at their mothers' udders; when celandines are showing like golden guineas in ditches; and daisies take the place of hailstones on every grass-warm bank. I see it at midsummer, when male stonechats perch on prickly sun-yellow gorse bushes; when rabbits, big and little, scuttle for shelter in all directions; when stoats are as fat on land as mackerel are fat in the sea; and when at night the moon irradiates each salty samphire plant balanced high up on the sea cliffs, on the lofty lonely faces of those chalk cliffs that, motionless as the sheeted sails of phantom ships, spell-bound, becalmed, flatly front the midnight waves. I see it again at the time of the autumn storms when rushing gales silence the moaning of the Shambles lightship, when weed and bent, by constant friction of their waving stalks, stand loosely in tiny round holes of mud, stand nodding and beckoning to the east in a frenzy of petulant penitence. I see it when foxes prowl in the twilight against the skyline, when Weymouth Bay, evening after evening, is lashed to fury, and seaside children, looking towards Portland through dismal window panes, begin to cry.

> The children look through the uneven pane
> Out to the world, to bring them joy again;
> But only snow flakes melting into mire
> Without, within the red glow of the fire.

The happiness of life does not depend on power, still less on possessions. I have seen in my time as many merry tramps as merry traders. What did Bacon say three hundred years ago? 'Money is like muck, it does most good when it is spread about'. With love in our hearts and bread and water in our bellies we shall do well enough. If a man keeps close to the ground and close to nature he will not go far out of the way.

But it is not only to the Dorset seaside that my mind flies in hours of distress. How many happy days it remembers spent in Dorset woodlands, in the Honeycombe Woods, in the Lulworth Woods, in the Came Woods! In such 'unspeakable rural solitudes' it is possible for lovers to store away wisdom that is as simple as sunshine. The ferns are never false, the fairy-tale foxgloves never fickle, and every warbler in the thicket sings madrigals of sweet delight, of the sweet days of summer time.

When a man is harried, hustled and hard driven by fate he will get small relief by bringing back to his mind the clamour and clutter of modernity. It is to the quiet pastoral places of his childhood, of his youth, that his thoughts had best be turned, dwelling in memory upon the long green lanes he knows, where, from the hedges on autumn afternoons, Sunday walkers pull down briony berries and straggling wreaths of old man's beard; upon patient sheep-washing pools, with little ferns pressing out from between masonry side-by-side with elbow-crooked herb-Robert; upon sequestered field ponds where narrow willow leaves float, listlessly adhering to the bark of old black sticks awkwardly protruding out of dark stagnant waters; upon ivy-bound walls under mossy sparrow-tunnelled thatch, where an old domesticated sheep-dog dozes away the slow passing hours, and the last peacock butterflies frivolously congregate in quest of chill morsels of Michaelmas nectar.

The Parson of Broadwindsor

I have often marvelled to remember how many novels of Sir Walter Scott my mother was able to read through to my father during a single winter. Winter evenings at the end of the last century seemed more substantial than they do today. If ever in my old age I enjoy again such solid intervals of time I have promised myself to read through from the beginning to the end the works of Thomas Fuller.

There are many men of letters who judge that England's finest prose belongs to the seventeenth century, and excepting perhaps Robert Burton and Sir Thomas Browne, no writing represents the weight and wit of that century's style better than does the prose of Fuller. What wisdom is contained in these 'golden works', to use Charles Lamb's happy phrase! What an honest divine is here, packing every sentence with as many shining conceits as a dorser's ped might be packed with John Dorys and writing always in a homely, racy language such as can be understood by all!

Thomas Fuller was born in 1608, the son of the Rector of Aldwincle, a village situated not far from Lilford Hall in Northamptonshire. The Rectory, a notable Elizabethan building, was, I am ashamed to say, demolished a hundred years ago by the Powys family.

Fuller's works should be of especial interest to us in Dorset, because for several years he held the living of Broadwindsor in this county. It was there that he wrote his *History of the Holy Warre* and *The Holy State and the Profane State*. It was there he married 'Eleanor'. It was there also that his eldest son John was born and baptised. He left the village soon after the outbreak of the Civil War, for, as Coleridge says, he was above everything 'a King's man'.

Loyalty was in his bones, loyalty to his king and loyalty to God. Of all the cavalier parsons he was the most honest. In truth, his natural piety was so strong that it caused him, in spite of his devotion to Charles, to favour on every possible occasion during the 'broken times' calm and moderate councils. The tolerant tone of his sermons soon became an offence to the supporters of the crown, and even his spirited conduct at the sieges of Basing House and Exeter did not quite succeed in wholly reinstating him in their confidence.

When we remember the kind of 'good thoughts' constantly entertained by Thomas Fuller we can easily understand how he would be suspected by the men of both parties who wished to settle their disputes by the sword. 'If I should chance to be stricken dumbe, I would with Zacharia make signs for table books and write that the name of that which I desire above all earthly things is Peace.' To those who reproached him during the Civil War for not completing his long-promised History of the Church, he made the following characteristic answer: 'I had little list or leisure to write history, fearing to be made history and shifting daily for my safety. All that time I could not live to study, who did only study to live.'

No sermon of his was ever dull. The Jacobean pulpit from which he preached still stands in the Broadwindsor church. Among his congregation were relations of Sir Francis Drake, but for the most part he preached his 'living homilies' to farmers, dairy men, labourers, blacksmiths, saddlers, carpenters who, as the years passed, became deeply attached to the good-hearted, whimsical, broad churchman. He taught them that African Negroes were not by any divine ordinance slaves, but rather 'images of God cut in ebony'.

He exhorted them to be understanding and tolerant and not to expect absolute perfection here on earth. 'A Church and a Reformation will be imperfect; do the best you can... this was a truth before your cradle was made and will be one after your coffin is rotten.' He had a word for the rich: 'As hills, the higher, the barrenner; so men, commonly the wealthier, the worse; the more Honour, the less Holinesse'. He reminded them that the civil commotions of England were being closely observed. 'The eye of all Christendom is upon us; the sea surrounds but doth not conceal us'. Some apposite apophthegm is to be found in every page he writes. 'All truths,' he says, 'have Eagles' eyes'.

Thomas Fuller first conceived the idea of his great masterpiece, *The Worthies of England*, while in Dorset. The book, however, was unfinished at the time of his death nearly thirty years later. It was eventually edited and published by his son John. It is the most entertaining, instructive and frolicsome of all Fuller's works. In it he enumerates the distinctions of each of the English shires, not forgetting to mention the several commodities they provide. Cambridgeshire, he asserts, is celebrated for 'eels, hares and willows'; Bedfordshire for 'barley, malts, fullers-earth and larks'; Hampshire for 'red deer, honey, wax and hogs'; Lancashire for 'oates and oxen and fair women'. The last 'commodity' prompts his quaint mind to the following reflection:

> Let the females of the county know that though in the Old Testament express notice be taken of many women, a) Sarah, b) Rebekah, c) Rachel, d) Tamar, e) Abishag, f) Esther; yet in the New Testament no mention at all is made of the fairness of women, soul-piercing perfection being far better than skin-deep fairness.

As might be expected he writes with a marvellous appreciation of Dorset. He finds it especially famous for its 'tenches, pipe clay and hemp'. The first commodity is to be found in the river Stour, the second near Poole and the third about Bridport. He declares with pride that Dorset can, 1) 'Feed itself with fine wheat, fat flesh, dainty fowl, wild and tame, fresh fish from sea and rivers'. 2) 'Clothe itself with its own wool and broadcloth made thereof; and it is believed that no place in England affordeth more sheep in so small a compass as this county about Dorchester.' 3) 'Build its own houses with good timber out of Blackmore Forest and with free-stone out of Portland ... nor wanteth it veins of marble in the Isles of Purbeck.'

Of the tench he writes: 'Plenty hereof are bred in the River Stour, which is so much the more observable, because generally this fish loveth ponds better than rivers, and pits better than either. It is a fish very pleasant in taste and is called by some the physician of fishes: though in my opinion it may better be styled the surgeon; for it is not so much a disease as a wound he cureth; nor is it any potion but a plaster which he affordeth; viz, his natural glutinousness which quickly consolidateth any green gash in any fish. But the pike is principally beholden unto him for cures of that kind; and some have observed that that tyrant, though never so hungry, forbeareth to eat this fish, which is his physician; not that pikes are capable (which many men are not) of gratitude; but that they are endued with a natural policy, not to destroy that which they know not how soon they may stand in need of.'

Fuller mentions Sherborne Castle and Lulworth Castle as being the two most consequential country seats in Dorset. On Dorset manor houses in general he offers the following remarks: 'The houses of the gentry herein are built rather to be lived in than to be looked on; very low in their situation (for warmth and convenience). Indeed the rhyme holds generally true of English structures,

The north for greatness, the east for health;
The south for neatness, the west for wealth.'

He observes that both Lulworth and Sherborne Castles escaped 'pretty well in the late war' and adds, not perhaps without a dash of malice, 'so that they have cause neither to brag nor complain'.

He cites three Dorset proverbs. 1) "As much a-kin as 'Lewson Hill' to Pilsen-Pen". That is, no kin at all. These two high hills, the first wholly, the other partly in the parish of Broadwindsor, whereof once I was minister. Yet, reader, I assure thee, that seamen make the nearest relation betwixt them, calling the one the cow and the other the calf; in which forms, it seems they appear first to their fancies, being eminent seamarks to such as sail along these coasts ...' 2) "'Stabb'd with a Bridport dagger"; that is, hanged or executed at the gallows; the best, if not the most, hemp growing about Bridport, a market town in the county ...' 3) '"Dorsetshire dorsers". Dorsers are peds, or panniers carried on the backs of horses on which hagglers used to ride and carry their commodities ... Fish jobbers bring up their fish in such contrivances above a hundred miles from Lime to London.'

Thomas Fuller supplies an abbreviated and not very satisfactory list of the 'gentry of the county'. He also enumerates the High Sheriffs from the reign of Henry II to Stuart times. Amongst these are to be found representatives of many well-known Dorset families—Frampton, Herring, Russel Williams (of Herringstone), Turbevil (of Bere), Trenchard (of Wolfeton), Martin, Strangways, Brown (of Frampton), Hussey (of Shopwick), Hening (of Pokeswell), Ashley (of St Giles), Bingham (of Melcombe).

His last piece of writing consisted of verses entitled 'A Panegyrick to His Majesty on His Happy Return'. He was not destined to enjoy the reign of his beloved prince for long. He had received from his patron, Lord Berkeley the living of Cranford in Middlesex, and it was here that he was buried in August 1661, after contracting a fever while preaching in London. His epitaph contains a graceful reference to his unpublished *Worthies of England*: 'While he was endeavouring to give immortality to others he himself attained it'.

Gypsies at Weymouth Market

It is a strange thing how the hearts of the least imaginative of us can be stirred by a sudden glimpse of gypsies. The undefined interest that we feel in seeing them at the end of a grassy lane or trekking in their ancient manner along one of our shining turnpike roads can be explained, I believe, by the fact that there is scarcely a person who does not envy them their entire freedom from the restraints of convention.

The life of the gypsies exemplifies the physical and spiritual emancipation that our ancestors enjoyed before they agreed, for the sake of security, to those social contracts that now so strictly regulate our lives. The gypsy tribes have never permitted the Tables of the Law to weigh heavily upon them. They do not give a rush or a cherry stone for those grave moral codes which so intimidate the rest of us.

The other day I went into the market at Weymouth to see if I could buy some good eating pears. As I stood waiting to be served I caught sight of two of these foreign women standing at the end of the building near the penny-in-the-slot machines. Whenever I see gypsies I am set marvelling at the racial tenacity that has preserved the identity of these Ishmaelites from northern India through so many centuries. There they stood, these two refugees from the fury of Tamberlaine, in Weymouth market, as though, with their shining teeth, their straight black hair, and sun-tanned foreheads they had only yesterday left those wide, hot plains over-shadowed by the Himalayas.

I made my way through the people to where they waited, these two magical phoenix birds settled for a moment amongst God's domesticated poultry. One of the women carried a baby in her arms. It was in no way troubled by the babble of voices that rose from the stalls, but was sleeping soundly. I looked at its round countenance with absorbed interest. Its black eyelashes, remarkable for their length, lay still upon its soft cheeks that were of the colour of old yellowed ivory.

There is a story that the Buddha was born under the palm tree. 'Suddenly came the infant Gotama and lay,' so runs the beautiful legend, 'like a jewel (the cat's eye) on muslin', while forthwith there fell from heaven upon the happy Maia a silver rain. This morsel of mahogany that I looked down upon might very well have been so blessed a child, an infant whose gentle wisdom might have been destined to bring consolation to the sad hearts of mortals more numerous than the grains of sand on the sea shore.

I asked the name of the baby. It was a girl and I learned that its name instead of being Devayani was Violet. There was something to me very touching about the incongruity of so innocent an English name having been selected for this little natural creature born beneath the waving dusky branches of a Dorset fir.

Yet, however these nomads try to identify themselves with the ways of Christendom their manners betray them. To this day gypsy girls are content to go in rags if they can indulge their Asiatic taste for gay jewellery. Like magpies they are attracted by what glitters, and who has not known them to discard a serviceable warm garment for one that is of a bright colour?

When they first began to appear in England at the beginning of the sixteenth century their leaders announced with the utmost gravity that they were 'Counts of lytel Egypt', their present designation being a testimony to that extremely characteristic initial prevarication.

They have always been hated and persecuted by householders. George Borrow declares that the gibbets of England have creaked and groaned with the corpses of gypsies. There are, however many songs and lilts and ballads that go to show the fascination these raggle-taggle Bedouins of our lanes and commons have had for restless dissatisfied girls of every generation:

> Ah, come away, says Johnny Faa,
> Ah, come away my dearie;
> And I dare swear by my ashen stave,
> Your Lord shall ne'er come near thee.

It is sad to see at the present time how our practical, matter-of-fact councillors make less and less allowance for these picturesque hedge rogues. Seldom now do we hear of a magistrate or great landlord who takes a benevolent interest in the gypsies and their affairs. They will seize upon any excuse to evict them from their traditional camping grounds. Yet I often think that these 'gypoos' understand the art of life better than the magnates themselves, with their convention-ridden lives. Many of us dissipate our emotional capacity with a succession of artificial sensations, whereas the gypsies are satisfied, like the animals, merely to be alive and feel the worshipful sun warm upon their skins.

When one sees them come straggling through the streets of Weymouth in early May with baskets full of bluebells and pink campions it is as refreshing to one's winter spirits as is the note of the first chiff-chaff. They treat the flowers carelessly and naturally, as children treat flowers and bear well in mind that nothing is more lucky than to buy for a piece of silver such a nosegay of Priapus with the cool dew of the Came Woods or Two Mile Copse still upon it.

I remained for some time talking to these two nut-brown girls. It happened that I had that afternoon purchased a bracelet in an old curiosity shop. It was made of a string of stones shaped like scarabs and in gratitude for the fact that I had been still able, even in our gross industrial age, to talk with authentic gypsies I gave the trinket to the mother to keep till her changeling daughter grew as tall as the bracken.

I asked where the baby had been born and the answer that the mother made me could hardly have failed to touch the heart's root of any son of Dorset whose spirit was not entirely corrupted, not entirely dead to the poetry and romance of life—Culliford Tree.

Betsy Cooper

Inextricably interwoven with the memories of my early childhood were the figures of Nancy and her daughter Betsy Cooper. Nancy must have been a very old woman then. Her age was beyond the reckoning powers of anyone in the village. Her face was one mass of wrinkles which fell in large white folds over her cheeks. We used to see her when we went out for nursery walks. Sometimes we would see her figure bending down to pick up sticks in the Park as we raced round the perambulator looking about on the sodden ground for the great sycamore leaves which in November took to themselves such wonderful colours.

In the spring time when the first dog violets came out and the daffodils were beginning to flower in the Battlefield, we would meet her far out in the country lanes returning from the back door of some country house where she had been begging. 'There goes thik old witch Nancy Cooper,' the village boys would shout as she trailed along the roads white for the first time for so many months with summer dust. There was a kind of cave on the side of Ham Hill called Johnny Cooper's Hole, and we used to be told by our nurse that Nancy had been born there. Whether this was true or not I don't know, but it all added to the romantic legendary conception with which our imaginations surrounded the old woman. The village people gave her scraps; they did not care to refuse them to one whose evil eye they feared.

'Good morning,' they would say, as she hobbled past their doors with a great hedge stick in her hand mumbling a salutation without looking up. She was dressed in rags, fold upon fold, and dirty garments covered her withered limbs and on her feet were ugly boots down at the heel and broken.

When I grew up it was her daughter Betsy that fascinated me. When I met her in the fields or lanes I would always try to get into conversation with her so that I might if possible learn something of the life and thoughts of this strange lonely figure who lived in so isolated a way. Once I met her in a field path that runs from Wulham's Mill to the turnpike road. It was in early June and her boots were covered with buttercup dust. It was a lovely day and the old woman seemed to appreciate it. She carried a bunch of lilacs in her hand which she had probably picked from some overgrown cottage hedge. 'Pretty, pretty,' she said, holding them up to me. ''Tis a-terrible happy to be out and traipsing in the spring time when the cuckoo be holloaing from 'en trees.' I told her that I thought so too, and then went on to talk of other matters.

''Folks do often look ugly to old Betsy,' she said. 'But there bain't be no bad looks in the meads where the flowers do grow. 'Tis always the folks—'twere the same with out blessed Lord—how badly they did serve Him.' I agreed again, wondering in my mind how strange a matter it was that the ill behaviour of a parcel of Jews in that long-ago time should have possibly been remembered by that old woman in the hayfields of England. After this I used to talk to her often, even visiting her house on one occasion and sitting with her while she poured me out black tea from a cracked pot. 'Bless 'ee, bless 'ee, my son,' she would say, 'thee be a pretty gentleman.'

Then I went to Africa for five years and heard no more of her, but sometimes as I rode across the dry veldt under the equatorial sun I would recall her figure and say to myself, 'I will certainly visit Betsy when I get back'; in a certain way she had become symbolic in my mind of all the English countryside in summer and autumn and winter. At last I was back again, and meeting the country doctor I asked him of news of Betsy. 'She was taken last week to the workhouse,' he said. 'The War has made it hard for beggars, and the village guardians have become strict.'

The next day I went to the great stone building where all the derelicts of society are hidden away from the eyes of the more favoured. I was led down a bleak passage and into a desolate ward. There on the bed lay Betsy Cooper very still and very pale. I think she recognised me for she kept repeating the words, 'You come home, you come home', and then suddenly she began complaining. 'I b'aint allowed no more to pick up they little sticks, or get a bite for me supper, or hear the cuckoos holloa. Folks have served me terrible bad, and I mid die now in thik girt home.' And the next week she died and was buried without sign or cross in a pauper's grave amongst nettles and rusty pieces of tin.

The Swannery Bell at Abbotsbury

There are many odd objects in Dorset which, though of no intrinsic value in themselves, might yet conceivably be treasured by the older inhabitants of the county, simple objects which have through the passing of years gathered to themselves happy associations. Of such inconspicuous Dorset objects the bell that admits visitors into Lord Ilchester's Swannery at Abbotsbury might take a place. Which of us has not stood impatiently at the familiar postern awaiting the moment when we would step out of an ordinary English hayfield into a garden of smooth tropical lawns overshadowed by waving reeds, lawns offering glimpses of inlets and lagoons where shining surfaces might, so it seems, at any moment be disturbed by a hippopotamus protruding a bristled chin out of the brackish water.

When I lived in Africa my mud hut used to be overgrown the year round with geraniums, and all through the hours, in the hot sunshine, humming birds with feathers as bright and varied as flowers used to keep darting and quivering against the broad leaves and gay petals of the sun-loving plants. This was a sight calculated to rouse the dullest spirit to a vibrant awareness of earth-existence, a sight, however, not more worshipful than the one I was once shown in this Dorset reserve—a reed warbler's nest suspended by delicate cables between two rushes swaying in the wind.

It is difficult to share the popular enthusiasm over the celebrated decoy. Most surely the contrivance testifies to the ingenuity of the human mind, but there is little joy to be derived from contemplating the initial treachery, and still less the culminating confusion at the decoy's end with its subsequent massacre of so many free, night-flying migratory birds. I have always admired the short stories of Guy de Maupassant. This great Frenchman wrote of life without fear. As a young man I especially appreciated the more erotic of his tales, so full of salt and cynicism. Once, as I idly turned over a collection of his works my notice was arrested by a story that had for its title the single word 'Love'. I began reading it—and behold the passion which this imaginative realist was treating was no human passion. The story described two sportsmen going out in the fens to shoot wild duck on an early winter's morning. The keen east wind, the distant booming of the contracting ice, the crisp ground, all were clearly evoked, but especially the devotion of a drake for his shot mate, as he fearlessly circled nearer and nearer to the guns over the place where she lay mortally wounded. This then is what I had happened upon instead of harlotry, and this story I regard as one of the most moving I have ever read. I was reminded of it when in Africa I saw a stallion zebra trotting around the dead body of his mare to keep the vultures away, which, in disconsolate rows, were sitting about the striped carcass.

I have been told that the two swans generally to be seen on the lawns at Abbotsbury have been together in content for many years, neither of them, so strong is the love they feel the one for the other, having known what it is to be restless though the sun shine never so bright on a spring morning. Mr Ernest Moule once told me that in China the fidelity of birds is so highly appreciated that it is the custom of the country to carry a goose before every bridal party, the ancient inhabitants of our farmyards being regarded in the Far East as a veritable symbol of matrimonial felicity. We in England are more accustomed to think of the goose as an emblem of folly. Chaucer, wishing to show how the tongue of a woman can extricate her from any situation, however awkward, makes her say:

24

Al had a man seen a thing with both his eyes
Yet shall we wymmen visage it hardly,
And wepe, and swere, and chide subtilly,
So that ye man schall be as lewd as gees.

The word 'lewd' is here used in its original meaning of ignorant, the passage suggesting that men, even in the face of the evidence of their own eyes, shall still, because of the brazen effrontery of women, remain ignorant as to what is taking place.

What a proud and sovereign bird is a swan! And how romantic the sound that comes from them in their passage across the Lodmoor sky in midwinter, their outstretched necks obedient to an infallible compass! When I was last in Weymouth I directed my bath-chair man to take me to the backwater that I might observe the swans at my leisure. Small wonder this bird has been a delight to poets from the earliest ages, and easy it is to understand how Leda allowed herself to be betrayed.

The Swannery at Abbotsbury is interesting to visit through all the summer months, though perhaps most so in the mating season. It is true, however, that swans on the land lose much of their majesty, the shortness of their legs giving them something of a waddling gait. This fact did not escape Chaucer's observant eye, and he hits off his roguish monk thus: 'Like Jovynian, Fat as a whal, and walken as a swan.'

It is a deplorable commentary upon the insensibility of our race that neither beauty of form nor grace of spirit has ever preserved any edible creature from our curious, shameless and insatiable appetites. The swan-herd on one of my visits pointed out to me a number of cygnets that were being nourished on a special diet 'for his Lordship's table'. So it has ever been. Swans, larks—into our pots they must go, and God bless them!

Now certainly he was a fair prelate;
He was not pale as a forpyned ghost,
A fat swan loved he best of any roast.

It does us more honour to remember the inspired works of laudation that our poets have given to this superb bird. Ben Jonson in his famous song to the Goddess of Love writes:

Have you seen but a bright lily grow

Before rude hands have touch'd it?
Have you mark'd but the fall of the snow
Before the soil hath smutch'd it?
Have you felt the wool of beaver
Or swan's down ever?

And Edmund Spenser has made, of course, the spectacle of swans on the Thames immortal:

So purely white they were,
That even the gentle streame, the which they bare
Seem'd foule to them, and bad his billowes spare
To wet their silken feathers, least they might
Soyle their fayre plumes with water not so fayre.

When I was taken as a very small boy to wait outside the Swannery door I was reminded, I remember, of a picture in one of my nursery books, and this 'Beauty and the Beast' association always comes back to me when I have occasion to refer to the Swannery. Yet how different it actually was from my fancies, when, our ringing at last answered, we were admitted into the Beast's garden! In the distance were innumerable forms in dazzling white as though a host of angels with folded wings were gathered upon the grass banks of the River of Life!

Dorset Ovens

The French cooks can with a persuasive touch handle saucepans, frying pan, grills and ovens more effectively than those of the same employment in other nations. They have a saying, 'Man is a born roaster'. This of course is far from the truth, for our primitive ancestors for unnumbered millennia knew nothing of the cooking trade, subsisting entirely upon raw leaves, raw roots, raw eggs, raw caterpillars and raw meat. In Dorset, however, it would actually be true to say that cooking was coincident with the first civilisation that we know anything about. During the recent excavations on Maiden Castle the most ancient object found was an oven, now to be seen at the County Museum at Dorchester. It is the original fire-pot, the father of all those thousands and thousands of fire pots that have brought content and good spirits to succeeding generations of men and women in Dorset.

How much good food has been cooked in the land of the Durotriges since this honest receptacle was in active use! The wisps of smoke 'a-twisten blue' that drift so lightly over our cottages, roofed 'wi' thatch as yellow as the yew', indicate clearly enough how important a part of our lives our 'firing cupboards of iron' have become. This same crooked smoke that floats into the sky from the high chimneys of our manor houses and from our signed village tuns might be taken to represent, as it were, an incense of life-worship that rises each day to the gates of heaven.

Not so long ago I visited the Swannery at Abbotsbury and, remarking upon some birds in particularly good case, was told by the swan-herd that they would presently be ready for his Lordship's table! The same afternoon I was entertained for tea in a nearby cottage where a black pudding was preparing for the evening meal. The contrast between the two dishes suggested Mediaeval days, well-busted egrets for the dietary of Lord Ilchester and 'swine's wine', made tasty with bread crumbs, for his humble villein.

For centuries after centuries the pig has supplied nourishment to the labourers of Dorset. I myself have scraped up bone fragments of this animal in a Bronze Age midden, while the following lines, out of Chaucer, go to show how hog's flesh has always been a national food:

> The bitter frosts with the sleet and reyn,
> Destroyed hath the green in every yerd
> Janus sit by the fyre, with double beard
> And, drinketh of his bugle-horn the wyne,
> Before his stant the brawn of tusked swyne,
> And 'Nowel' cryeth every lusty man.

If I were to be asked what particular food was characteristic of Dorset I should suggest mutton, though the celebrated Portland breed (albeit Portland lamb is still sold in London markets) has for a long time become extinct, the last flock being owned by Squire Goodden of Fleet House. Next to Dorset mutton I would say Blue Vinny cheese, a variety coloured by fen or blue mould and which, though difficult now to come by except in outlying farms, is considered by many to be cheese far superior to all others in the royal realm of England. Thomas Fuller who for many years held the Dorset living of Broadwindsor used to commend very highly the tench of Dorset which is a fish still plentiful in the upper reaches of the River Stour. The tench is distinguished by a solemn deportment and a grave countenance and was rumoured by the ancients to be the physician of the fishes, and on account of this the pike were said never to molest it, not so much, as is explained by Fuller, 'out of gratitude' as from 'a natural policy, not to destroy that which they knew not how soon they might stand in need of'.

Though the rich water-meadows that lie along the Stour valley provide fat grazing for wonderful herds of warm-breathing dairy cows, yet we in Dorset seldom like to trouble to scold our cream as is the practice further west. Our tastes are simple and we prefer to meddle as little as possible with our food. We leave sophisticated dishes, and clotted trifles for our town cousins, all our own cry being for 'dunch-puddens'.

Yet in spite of our protests in favour of plain cooking, if anyone should smell the sweet savours that rise from the loaded tables of our Sunday meat dinners they would appreciate the fact that between Sherborne and Poole and Lyme Regis, there are thousands of men and women who excel in the most valuable of all culinary arts, the art of doing ordinary everyday dishes 'to a turn'. I am not now referring to those receipts that especially belong to the county, such as Portland dough cakes where lard is put to the best possible use, Bridport knobs, a biscuit unrivalled in the west, girdle- or griddle-cakes and dried mackerel which supplies the villages behind the Chesil Beach with their staple winter diet and which prepared in various ways serves as sound victuals for the lively lusty fishing folks of Deadman's Bay. Though it would be an exaggeration to report us as gross eaters in Dorset we could safely be styled healthy trencher-men, in winter-time spending many hours of the day 'with our bellies to the table and our backs to the fire', there being taken up at each meal food sufficient to keep plump a dozen or more white Wyandot capons.

Two years ago a brother of mine—a sheep-farmer from Africa—came to England on a visit. He was invited to look over the stock of my good neighbour Farmer Cobb of West Chaldon. It was the month of May and they had arranged to meet at five o'clock in the morning. The sun was shining brightly on the broad new leaves of the sycamore and the cuckoos were calling and calling by the time my brother reached the old farm. He found his host in the barton yard 'as dapper as a dunnick'. This old-fashioned Dorset farmer immediately pressed him to step inside for a moment to have a 'bite of summat', and my brother presently found himself with a plate of cold beef before him as tender, or to use an old Dorset word, as 'nish' a piece of meat as he had ever eaten.

Anybody who has lodged for a summer in a Dorset farmhouse will give high praise to our women. They are wise enough to know that a full pot keeps a house happy and that there is nothing better than a good pasty plaster to mend a sullen face:

> An' if you look'd 'ithin their door
> You zee em in their pleace,
> A-doen house wirk up avore
> Their smilen mother's feace;
> You'd cry—'Why, if a man would wive
> An' thrive, 'ithout a dow'r,
> Then let en look en out a wife
> In Blackmore by the Stour.

One week it is the time for duck and green peas, the next week it is Whit Sunday and the little rosy-cheeked maid has supplied the cool larder with a large cooking basin of green fruit as hard as bullets, all ready, headed and tailed, for the first gooseberry tart. Now the weeks have come when the willow-pattern plates, grown dim with age and use, are piled high with broad beans in their grey coats! Then again it is the blackberry season and there stands on the sideboard a huge jug of fresh autumn cream to mix with the delicious juices of these 'wild grapes' that were gathered after school by the children of the village from long green hazel nut hedges. In conclusion I dare venture to say that it would be difficult to find any London food more delectable, more tasty than a breakfast mess of mushrooms, peeled with the beads of the downland dew still fresh upon them, and then fried upon toast until their delicate gills collapse to become crisp and black and laid upon hot fried bread. There is need only to recall such simple pleasures of the table to have our steadfast belief confirmed that as long as a man can put meat into his mouth life is to be prized.

Lodmoor

For a whole year after the Great War I slept every night in the garden of a ruined cottage that used to stand on the crest of a hill a mile or two eastward from Weymouth. The hill is known as Jordan Hill and was the place where the Roman marine resort named Clavinium was once situated.

In a corner of the neglected garden was a well which must have supplied the daughters of Dorset with many a bucketful of fresh water.

> This Emeleye with herte debonaire
> Hir body wessh with water of a welle.

And in another corner stood a thorn tree bent double by south-western gales. Across the sloping stubble field where once flocks of November finches, with shining wings, swerved in unison, there runs now a wide modern road used all day long by commercial vans supplying the needs of the prosperous householders of a pleasant suburb. I understand that all trace of the derelict cottage garden has long since been obliterated, the site which my shelter once occupied amongst docks, nettles, and brambles, having been transformed into a civilised lawn, upon which on summer evenings genial burgomasters sip their wine, contemplating their Royal West Country watering-place curving southward like the silver bow of Apollo, and the sunset behind the primitive landscape of Lodmoor with its hint of a fading and infinite past.

On one occasion when I was walking back to Weymouth from the deserted garden I overtook two boys. It was on a late winter's afternoon and I was not able to see their faces, but overheard one of them saying to the other, evidently a newcomer to the district, 'That is Lodmoor. *It is a fine place.*' The last words were spoken with so enthusiastic an emphasis that I recognised this schoolboy as already initiated into the secret fascination of this ancient fen, which has always exercised a strong influence upon Dorset people. For the proximity of the open marshland has generously contributed to the health and happiness of the townsfolk of Weymouth; supplying the commonalty with a sporting reserve of their own and people who prize the quiet of nature with a ready escape from the seaside crowds.

Lodmoor possesses a singular character of its own. This may be partly explained by the fact that is has always divided its allegiance between sea and land, drawing equally from the two sources for the appeal of its desolation. Its wide wild acres have offered a habitat for unfamiliar flowers, and the banks of its ruddy dykes are continually frequented by rare birds.

Although blood-sports are at all times and in all places to be deplored, deriving their excitement as they do out of the unregenerate gratification of gross animal impulses unworthy of sensitive and mature beings, they are more easily forgiven when they are indulged in by hungry men who shoot for the pot. In the old days when the poor of Weymouth were allowed free access to these marshlands, jersey-wearing sportsmen were content to wait for hours in the bitterest winds on the chance of supplying a cottage kitchen down by the harbour with a plump widgeon.

How wonderful Lodmoor could be on a Christmas-week morning, when it was still dark and the contracting ice sent booming reverberations along the waterway, and each bulrush and thin pennanted reed was furred with a silver filigree, and the bay and the shelving beach and the white turnpike house, with its heaped piles of backyard pinewood, were all lying white and calm through the last slow hour before the breaking of the dawn.

And yet perhaps it is in the spring-time that Lodmoor is most beautiful. The little uncomplaining servant-girls who early every morning garnish so dutifully the doorsteps of the Brunswick Terrace lodging houses have hardly had time to notice the first squill showing blue in their mistress's railed-in front garden before the spring is already fully present on Lodmoor, with clumps of gawdy kingcups opening to the sun, with the first swallows skimming over the fast-drying ox-paddled flats, and the first cuckoo calling from the Horse-shoe spinney of South Down Farm.

As I write there hangs over my bed a little water-colour of just such a scene as I describe, with White Nose and the renowned chalk cliffs clearly visible in the distance. The picture was painted by my sister a quarter of a century ago. We had noticed some wild cattle on the causeway known as 'the Pipes', so for safety we had left her on an island with her paint-box while my brother and I went off to look for red-shanks' nests; and although in after years in Africa it was the same brother who always protected me, saddling my ponies and shooting my lions, in these days I was the stronger, and able to carry him on my back across the shallower lagoons.

Though I have not seen a red-shank's egg for many years, I well remember the look of its dull stone colour, smutched with reddish brown. A red-shank is as subtle as a 'false lapwing' in its efforts to conceal the position of its nest, and every winter it must draw down upon its little grey cranium numberless curses from the men with guns, whose sporting prospects it has spoiled with the insistent cries of warning it emits from its long bill so charmingly tipped with scarlet.

Many rare creatures are to be seen on the wilder stretches of this Weymouth bird sanctuary. I remember one winter being told by old Tom Symonds, whose father had been a dairy man at Upwey, and who was as keen a naturalist as I have ever known, that he had been watching a whooper swan for more than a week on the Lodmoor water. Otters also have been disturbed by men crossing the marshlands early on summer mornings, this giant weasel appearing like a foreign beast, like a black velvet-coated beaver, as, scattering the dew from some patch of tall grass, it plunges into deep water.

My father in his old age used to find it difficult to summon words for the expression of his thoughts. On one occasion when he was walking across Lodmoor he suddenly stood still by the side of a waterway. He had happened to catch sight of an enormous eel, and with concentrated intelligent attention was watching the movements of the wriggling fish, as, with slow fins, it propelled itself over the reddle-stained mud at the bottom of the dyke. I have always admired my sister's description of this scene, her description of this mute old man who, even at that late end of his life, had never lost interest in the existence of other animal creatures, his familiar companions during the long tally of hours that make up the life of an octogenarian.

The Wordsworths in Dorset

Students of the life of William Wordsworth have always regarded the year and a half that he spent in Dorset of the greatest importance; for it was at Racedown that the poet first put to a practical test his native disposition for 'simple living and high thinking'.

His bastard daughter had been safely born, and his own attorney's son-good-sense had not only successfully disentangled him from Annette Vallon's life but had also modified his youthful ardour for revolution. With such disruptive emotions stilled, Wordsworth at the age of twenty-five was able to settle down to enjoy the passing of those quiet days that were to make up his long, happy and uneventful life.

It would be hard to find a man of letters as favoured by the Fates as was Wordsworth. De Quincey observes, not without a grain of envy and malice, that he had only to approach a state of anxiety about money to have his income augmented by some fresh good chance.

At the beginning of the year 1795 Raisley Calvert had died of consumption, leaving a legacy of £900 to Wordsworth. In a letter dated February 20th 1805, Wordsworth comments on this happening to Sir George Beaumont in the following manner: 'This bequest was from a young man with whom, though I call him friend, I had had but little connection, and this act was done entirely from a confidence on his part that I had powers and attainments which might be of use to mankind.'

The timely windfall enabled Wordsworth to give up the discouraging idea of trying to earn his living by everyday journalism. A Cambridge tutor, Mr Montagu, an illegitimate son of Lord Sandwich, introduced him to John Pinney, the son of a rich Bristol merchant, and this generous young spark who had been given Racedown for his own use suggested that the Wordsworths should take up their residence there rent free, though the business-like father was left to imagine that Wordsworth was paying a suitable sum for his tenancy. Dorothy Wordsworth has given us a description of this rich young man:

'He is two and twenty, has a charming countenance and the sweetest temper I ever observed. He has travelled a good deal, in the way of education, been at one of the great schools and at Oxford, has had always plenty of money to spend and every indulgence, all these things instead of having spoiled him or made him conceited have wrought the pleasantest and best effects, he is well-informed, has an uncommonly good heart, and is very agreeable in conversation.'

It was part of the arrangement that John Pinney should be allowed to come and stay for short visits at Racedown whenever the mood prompted him to do so. 'We have not gone on with our usual regularity,' records Dorothy at the end of his visit in the spring of 1796. She speaks of the youth's 'coursing', and to many of us it is sad to contemplate Wordsworth as being involved in this sport, sad to think of so barbarous a pastime taking place 'in the plain presence of his dignity', and we cannot but compare his acquiescence with the wild fury that possessed Robert Burns at seeing a mangled hare run past him:

> Inhuman Man! Curse on thy Barb'rous art,
> And blasted be thy murder-aiming eye;

36

May never pity soothe thee with a sigh,
Nor ever pleasure glad thy cruel heart!

In her money calculations Dorothy estimated that their income at Racedown would be £180 a year, a sum to be made up from dividends of the Calvert legacy, the lucky William finding he could get '9 per cent for the money upon the best security', and from £50 a year that Mr Montagu proposed to allow Wordsworth for boarding and looking after his little boy. Basil Montagu gravely testifies to the high value he put upon his friendship with Wordsworth. 'We spent some months together. He saw me with great industry perplexed and misled by passions wild and strong. In the wreck of my happiness he saw the probable ruin of my infant ... After some time he proposed to take my child from my chambers in London into Dorsetshire, where he was about to settle with his sister ... I consider having met William Wordsworth the most fortunate event of my life.'

Was it De Quincey who once had the audacity to ask Wordsworth, 'so singled out for his grave thoughts', why he had never written a poem on the ecstasy of love and was told that the subject was one that moved the poet too deeply for him to venture to give utterance to it in words? As a boy Wordsworth had entertained himself with dancing and playing with his country neighbours. At Cambridge he conducted himself with the moral levity of a young gentleman of his age, and we know how the beautiful Annette during his stay in France stirred his emotions out of all control. Possibly it was a certain North Country caution and stability of character that Montagu so highly commends, a shrewd sense of direction, that helped Wordsworth to steady the wayward conduct of his less prudent friend.

The brother and sister arrived at Racedown in November, driving from Bristol in a chaise with their little charge, Basil Montagu the second. Though for a long time used as a farmhouse Racedown Lodge is in reality a well-constructed 18th century small gentleman's country house. It stands in a sheltered dell of one of the foothills of Pilsden Pen on the north east side of the homely 'mountain'. To anyone who for the sake of leisure and freedom has lived poor in Dorset, adopting the short coat of the philosopher, the domestic economy of this household, nay the whole manner of life of brother and sister, is of especial interest. 'I am determined,' wrote Wordsworth on 7th November, 'to throw myself into that mighty gulph that has swallowed up so many, of talents and attainments infinitely superior to my own. One thing, however, I can boast, and on one thing I rely, extreme frugality. This must be my main support, my chief *vectigal*.' They found everything in the house in order so that they had not 'to lay out ten shillings' for the use of it. They employed a maidservant from the village—a Dorset girl named Peggy—whom they grew to appreciate so much that long after she had left their service to marry, and had gone to live at Lyme Regis, they used to send her money. They had a washing day once a month hiring a woman to whom they paid nine-pence; they dried the clothes the next day, and on the day following did the ironing. Dorothy herself acted as seamstress for the household making for Basil 'coloured frocks, shirts, slips, etc.', and keeping her brother William's clothes mended. Their provisions were brought from Crewkerne by their butcher. If we are to believe Wordsworth their diet was principally a vegetarian one, for in a letter to his friend Wrangham he writes, 'I have been lately living upon the air and the essence of carrots, cabbages, turnips and other esculent vegetables, not excluding parsley.' Coal they found very expensive. That this made an impression on Wordsworth is proved from his lines:

This woman dwelt in Dorsetshire,
Her hut was on a cold hill-side,
And in that country coals are dear,
For they come far by wind and tide.

and Dorothy writes to her friend Jane Marshall, 'You would be surprised to see what a small cart full we get for three or four and twenty shillings.'

Their theories about bringing up Basil were advanced for the end of the 18th century. 'We teach him nothing at present but what he learns from the evidence of his senses ... He knows his letters, but we have not attempted any further step in the path of *book-learning*. Our grand study has been to make him happy.' The boy was at first inclined to be fretful, and would often cry. Dorothy devised the plan of sending him into 'an apartment of tears' till he was again in a good humour. After a few days, whenever the child felt troubled, he would say, 'Aunt, I think I am going to cry,' and then go into his confinement of his own accord. 'We have no punishments except such as appear to be, as far as we can determine, the immediate *consequence* that is to grow out of the offence.'

They used to walk for about two hours every morning. The country about the two hills, Pilsdon Pen and Lewesdon, is sandy, which made it especially suitable for their favourite occupation. Every week they had to walk as far as Crewkerne for their letters, a distance of fourteen miles there and back. Dorothy admired the broom and gorse that grew under the firs of Lewesdon, and also the West Country orchards 'without any other enclosure or security than as a common field.' She pointed out to her friend that Racedown Lodge was situated at an equal distance from the towns of Crewkerne, Chard, Axminster, Bridport and Lyme, and stood only a field away from the Devonshire border marked by a brook 'untainted with the commerce of the world'. The stream must have been well-known to 'that old King's man', Thomas Fuller, who some hundred and seventy years before had held the living of Broadwindsor, the fine Jacobean pulpit from which he preached his 'good thoughts in bad times' being still used in the parish church. A few yards from the house the sea was visible 'through different openings of the unequal hills'. It was through one of these openings that Wordsworth one day watched 'the West Indian fleet sailing in all its glory before the storm had made such dreadful ravages.' Little did the poet know that ten years later the splendid merchantman, the *Earl of Abergavenny*, under the command of his brother Captain John Wordsworth, was to founder on the Dorset coast with the loss of many lives, the drowned body of the unfortunate captain, aged 32, eventually being washed onto Weymouth beach.

Walking, gardening and chopping wood were the forms of recreation most favoured by the poet. 'I have been,' he writes, 'an hour and a half this morning hewing wood and rooting up hedges, and I think it no bad employment to feel "the penalty of Adam".' Occasionally Wordsworth would go riding, and Miss M. Jourdain, who has written a valuable essay on 'The Literary Associates of Dorset', reports that they still tell in the tavern of Broadwindsor a story of how Wordsworth borrowed a horse from a neighbour to ride to Lyme Regis, and there having stabled it in the morning, forgot all about it and returned to the village as had been his usual custom on foot.

Perhaps the most memorable event that happened during their stay at Racedown was Coleridge's visit there in June of 1796. Wordsworth had already met Coleridge in Bristol but their friendship was confirmed under the trees of Dorset and in the parlour, 'the prettiest little room that can be', as they read their manuscripts in the evenings to each other, with the dew-damp scents of midnight hayfields drifting in through the open window along with the insistent garden moths that fluttered about their well-snuffed candles of tallow fat. 'I am sojourning a few days at Racedown,' wrote Coleridge to his friend Cottle, 'the mansion of my friend Wordsworth. He admires my tragedy, which gives me great hopes; he has written a tragedy himself. I speak with heartfelt sincerity, and I think unblinded judgement, when I tell you that I feel a little man by his side.' And truly what a meeting it must have been! Wordsworth was 26, and Coleridge was 24 years old. Ill-health had not yet dishonoured the younger man. They were both vigorous enough to be out in the fields 'before the mower was abroad among the dewy grass', talking, talking, talking, on and on and on, until the first star appeared in the evening sky! And what walks they took, those three excited friends, walks through Dorset lanes, odorous with warm intermittent puffs of mass honeysuckle tods, walks lasting from early in the afternoon 'until the light had failed, and ivy leaf and flower were lost into green hedges'.

It has been conjectured that Dorothy Wordsworth came to feel a particular tenderness for her brother's remarkable friend. She certainly gives us a valuable description of his appearance in those happy days before his distresses had fallen upon him with any great severity. 'He is a wonderful man. His conversation teems with soul, mind and spirit. Then he is so benevolent, so good tempered and cheerful, and like William, interests himself so much about every little trifle. At first I thought him very plain, that is, for about three minutes; he is pale and thin, has a wide mouth, thick lips, and not very good teeth, longish, loose-growing half-curling rough black hair. But if you hear him speak for five minutes you think no more of them. His eye is large and full, not dark but grey; such an eye as would receive from a heavy soul the darkest expression; but it speaks every emotion of his animated mind; it has more of the "poet's eye in a fine frenzy rolling" than I ever witnessed.'

It was at Racedown that Wordsworth wrote "The Ruined Cottage". This simple, beautiful Dorset poem is not incorporated in the first book of *The Excursion*. It is extremely characteristic of the manner of his genius.

I remember once asking my brother John what he considered to be the especial value of Wordsworth's poetry. He answered without hesitation that his greatest gift was his power of expressing the quality of patient endurance, like the endurance that belongs to mothers and to very old people. He reminded me of the poem "Resolution and Independence", where the leech gatherer is described standing over a pond 'moving altogether if he moved at all', and he went on to say that Wordsworth teaches us not to require beauty, or love, or passion, or glory, but to derive an old-animal sort of pleasure from the mere sensation of being alive, alive to feel the warmth of a cottage fire upon our knees, alive to feel the sun shining down upon the village street. In "The Ruined Cottage" the tragic sorrow of the deserted country woman is juxtaposed against the indifference of nature observed with the slow convincing realism so peculiar to Wordsworth. She earns a scant livelihood by the very West Dorset occupation of spinning hemp for the Bridport rope manufacturers; 'to die by a Bridport dagger' being a sly local reference to a death by hanging, as Fuller recalls. The woman's husband, distracted by poverty, has enlisted for the foreign wars. The forlorn mother, forever on the look-out for his unexpected return, gradually loses her wits. Without any industrious and careful master, the garden plot of the small cottage becomes derelict—the trees, the 'shining footstone' of the well—subject only to 'the soft handling of the elements', the very cottage door, visited 'familiarly' by the sheep from the neighbouring common, 'with dull red stains discoloured, and stuck o'er with tufts and hair of wool', and the matted weeds of the overgrown neglected garden':

> Marked with the steps of those whom, as they passed,
> The gooseberry trees that shot in long, lank slips,
> Or currants, hanging from their leafless stems
> In scanty strings, had tempted to o'er leap
> The broken wall.

Those of us who claim Dorset as our 'peculiar nook of earth', are proud to remember that William and Dorothy Wordsworth began their life together under Pilsdon Pen. The rare devotion that existed between the two remains a treasured memory in English literature. It lasted on even to those dolorous days when the light in Dorothy's 'wild eyes' became dimmed by mental disorders, so that her aged brother, eager to do her the least service, would be seen taking his place at her bedside to wash her feet. And we cherish the fact that in spite of the appeal of mountain and fell, of lake and cataract, Dorothy Wordsworth's deepest allegiance remained in Dorset. 'Racedown,' she once wrote, 'is the place dearest to any recollections upon the whole surface of the island; it was the first home I had.'

Birds of a Winter Garden

For eighteen months now I have been living in an open-air shelter and have been able to watch closely the ways of the common garden birds that come to feed from the contrivances suspended from the roof of my hut. The blackbird is always the first to wake, flying out of his roosting place with his cheerful clatter of feigned alarm, the same clatter that he enjoys making as he scuds towards his brambly roosting place in the November twilight.

The common sparrows and finches are seldom up and about until it is almost daylight. Of these smaller birds the hedge sparrows are awake earlier than any. They appear when the deep dusk of the vanishing night is still lingering upon the rain-drenched winter flower-beds. At such a time it is easy to mistake them for mice, so softly and silently do they move over the mould, with their little lowered heads intent already on the business of the day. There is a reserve of manner about these delicate creatures that is very winning. Their plumage corresponds exactly with their character. A person not interested in birds might well miss the beautiful slate blue about the neck and breast of the small fowl of the garden plot, but when once observed it is impossible not to apprehend the russet harmony of the precise feathers.

Never have I forgotten the excitement I experienced when first I saw a hedge sparrow's nest with its blue eggs. It was in a box tree, and I had to be lifted up before I could open the closely grown leaves sufficiently to look into the nest. I had never expected anything so perfect—the superbly formed blue eggs of the colour of the summer sky, of the colour of the summer sea, lying in their deep nest of woven moss and twigs so exquisitely lined with slippery horse hair. These birds usually stay close to each other all the year through, the male hardly distinguishable from the female, both dutifully performing their daily task of taking into their little bellies the dainty morsels most suitable for their fastidious tastes, insects and caterpillars in the summer, and seeds in the winter. Their plan of life is 'to go along quietly'. They are always ready to give place to more aggressive birds, content to wait until these ruder ones have snatched and grabbed and flown away before continuing their patient, particular searchings, gravely hopping over grass and gravel, one foot a little before the other.

The chaffinches also have an air of good breeding. They are, however, much more free and frolic. They derive their name from their love of frequenting places where they are likely to find a litter of chaff—the thresholds of barns, the ground below the swaying windlass hook of a mill, the flagged space outside a stable, the stone steps up to a granary, or a dovecote's open floor. If only they hop about long enough in such poetical places they are sure to find sooner or later a rewarding corn grain! Their song is utterly blithe.

> I have come down this fine morning
> To pick up a round piece of grain O!

If I have placed crumbs on the table at my bedside a chaffinch is sure to be the first to venture near. He will be careful, however, to announce his presence from a distance with his cry of 'pink, pink'. After I have looked up and he knows for certain that I have seen him he is reassured and will fly on to the table with no further to-do. His action in flight is deft and dancing and it is pretty to see how proudly he will sometimes arch his neck before alighting. What a change, too, comes over him in the springtime, for the plumage of the cock chaffinch on an April morning is as bright as a flower, as bright as the wings of a butterfly. How bold and brisk and exacting a lover he is to his little greenish mate, as he dances before her with shining epaulettes on each shoulder and rose pink breast 'as cheerful as a chaffinch'.

In my childhood I used often to see my mother, as she sat sewing in the dining room, move a chair that she might get a better view of the birds enjoying the crumbs she had thrown out of the tall French window. My brother and I were much preoccupied with our catapults and this, we knew, was a trouble to our mother. We kept our slugs in an unused tea-caddy on the dining-room sideboard and I remember on one occasion when I was surreptitiously securing out of it fresh supplies of ammunition, hearing her refer to the house sparrows with amused indulgence as representing the rabble or populace. This indeed was, and will for ever be the truth, for although it is in the nature of these crafty, parasitic little wretches to be extremely suspicious and trap-shy, when once they have gained confidence it is like having a crowd of noisy, undisciplined boys let into a secret garden.

I endeavour to reconcile myself to their conduct by remembering that I am looking upon life in action, natural and unregenerate, but try as I may I cannot regard them with enthusiasm. They come with a rush, invading every feeding place, the hens little less aggressive than the cocks. They scramble and fight. Continually I am startled by cries of real pain and look up to see one of these birds, with its black chops and heavy finch bill, crouched low in preparation for another and more deadly attack. Their behaviour is always offensive. What other bird, except perhaps a seagull depraved by the pressure of harbour-mouth conditions, has trained itself to swallow enormous pieces of food without a pause, gulp by gulp, as a snake swallows a frog? Yet, if you watch a number of house sparrows feeding it is easy to understand why they have learned this greedy trick. If one of the number happens to have found a good piece of food it is a recognized custom that he should be pursued in the hope of getting him to drop the envied morsel. No sparrow leaves a bird table with an appreciable mouthful without having five or six of his brothers flying at his tail.

Bewick in writing of the common sparrow delivers himself of the following homily: 'As the great table of nature is spread out alike to all' we must not 'grudge their scanty pittance' but indeed lift up our hearts 'in grateful effusions to Him "who filleth all things living with plenteousness".' For myself, after watching the behaviour of this adulterous generation of these sons of Belial for twelve months, Count de Buffon's judgement jumps more with my humour: 'The sparrow is extremely destructive, its plumage is entirely useless, its flesh indifferent food, its notes are grating to the ear, and its familiarity and petulance disgusting.'

My favourite of all the birds is the blue tit. It is as bright as a tropical bird, bold, resolute and expert in all its movements. The Revd John Newton once accused poor William Cowper of being too gay, 'of playing at archery and wearing a green coat'. For sure the poet's haberdasher was never able to supply him with a coat that could match the blue tit's debonair jacket so green and yellow of hue. A pair of blue tits always appears together in the autumn and stays with me until St Valentine's Day, when the notion somehow gets into their little craniums that a cottage garden in an undisturbed valley of the Dorset downs is no good place for nesting, and away they go to the Warmwell Woods, or to Lulworth where there are trees and walls.

It is only in the real cold weather that the starlings will come to the table. The starling is a bird that possesses little physical resistance. It chooses to die rather than to endure any great privation. In a cold spell I have been astonished to see how many of these clever birds will fall dead from their roosting branches. This autumn a white starling was in the neighbourhood for a month. It excited me to see it, whether strutting with its fellows on the rain-drenched downs as white as any goose-white seagull, or resting itself on a bare elder branch making me dream that a slip of the Glastonbury thorn had been planted amongst the gorse and was now in flower, or flashing by overhead with its whirling companions, an angel of light amongst a host of instinctive earth-borns.

Wrens I have never succeeded in feeding. I think when the frost kills the little spiders they love to eat they are put to desperate shifts for food. Last year one was caught by a cat cowering under the cabbages, too dazed evidently with hunger and cold to look out for itself. I don't wonder the smallest of all our birds has always fascinated our imaginations. Its barred feathers suggest a game bird, as does its cocked tail and quick secretive movements in and out of the branches. I could well imagine fairies of an unpleasant sort, about the size of a ploughman's spikenard and with the spirit of the chase still not outgrown, making much of wren shooting as a pastime, sending out leather-gaitered foresters to look for traces of them on the winter leaves much as in our world keepers will mark the 'chalk' of the woodcock on the soft mud where the stream winds its way through straggling undergrowth at the bottom of the covert.

The manners of the robin are not above criticism. His unabashed egoism is apparent to all, but then he has always been so faithful an ally to mankind, and his breast is so bright, and his back such a subtle colour that one is willing to forgive him his exaggerated sense of personal property. Besides, do we not know that these two garden birds, the robin by the window and the wren in the privet hedge, are both of them under divine patronage? Who could forget the old rhyme dinned into our ears as children?

> The Robin and the Wren
> Are God's cock and hen.

The Chesil Beach

With all the world menaced with war the writing trade is no easy one. In a letter to The Bodley Head I complained recently, referring to the publication of a new book, that it was like launching a paper boat from the Chesil Beach in a spring gale. No sooner had I put down the careless sentence, badly sporting as it did with the conventional tone suitable to a sensible business letter, than, in my protracted exile with my scalp all but scraping the ceilings of Heaven on the topmost Alps, I became suddenly obsessed with an overwhelming yearning to view once again that wonderful sea-bank which, not to be matched the world over, has from early prehistoric times obstinately resisted the raging winter furies of the Atlantic.

The Chesil Beach is truly a monument, created by Nature and bequeathed by her for the protection of Dorset, a monument curved like the bow of Cupid and embracing the West Bay as firmly and gracefully as a young man's arm turns about the waist of the maiden he loves. Very adroitly has this natural breakwater been built; at first with shingle sands small as millet seeds, which, increasing gradually in size as the great bank sweeps eastward, becomes under Portland magnified almost to the proportions of stick-house grindstones. It has been said that a Chesilton fisherman, even though he were blind, could tell his exact position along the whole span of the royal rampart by the simple process of handling the pebbles under his boots. This uniform variability of the congregated sea stones gives to the twenty-mile massive barrier a most singular property, none other than the gift of music, so that when the felon winds are up in wild weather, the long length of its curvature is, like a humming fiddle, capable of emitting very different notes, those down Bridport way sounding treble as the shrill shrieking of a covey of night-flying witches, and those nearer to Portland as gruff and forbidding as are the roarings of a pride of African lions, a resonance which, like the thunder of Poseidon, the earth-shaker, could reach, it would seem, to the world's end, and does, in actual fact, come drumming intermittently into the dutiful ears of shepherds watching over their lambing ewes on the Ridgeway Downs, or for that matter of poaching gypsies tramping back through the drenching rain to their caravan, camped at Culliford Tree.

I have often thought, if my fortunes should turn Turk with me, that I would like nothing better than to live on my old-age pension in an attic of The Cove Inn. This romantic tavern, washed bone-bare by rain and salty spindrifts, stands by itself on the Chesil Beach. It is a house frequented for the most part by sea-fishing men home for a holiday and local fishing folk. They must have merry times there, back from the seven seas, snug again with kinsmen and friends—Dorset longshoremen, who, on All-Hallows or on Christmas Eve or at Candlemas, in warm well-darned jerseys, sit drinking against the sea-coal fire in this sturdy habitation with walls of stone as rough as those of a medieval castle.

How lucky a lot for any old man to be a simple lodger in such a place, stepping out onto the shingly open-air barbican while the breakfast was being got ready, the tar-splashed pebbles scrunching under his heels as he avoids treading upon the brown nets that, with shimmering, mackerel scales still adhering to their meshes, have been—like dark gigantic spider webs—spread out to dry in the clear dancing sunshine of a summer's morning. There before him lies the unharvested water stretching away, visible and naked, as far as eye can reach, a huge azure mill pond, fit pasturing ground for a sea-serpent of hideous countenance or for the solacing of that leviathan we used to learn about in the Bible.

From the rocky promontories of the Bill, from the heathery heights, bracken-forested, around Hardy's Monument, from Golden Cap, with its prickly clumps of sea-blown, honey-smelling gorse, the seascape of the Chesil Beach appears equally noble in the pure outline of its memorable crescent, lovely in the lightness of its summer beauty with eryngo blue between its stones, and with the terns in the bright air darting and diving and crying, and awe-inspiring beyond imagination in the terrible seasons of its wrath. 'He that will learn to pray let him go to sea.'

Was it to The Cove Inn, I have often wondered, that the crew of the 90-ton stone-laden ordnance sloop, *Ebenezer*, first came to announce themselves, seamen saved by a miracle, their good ship left high and dry on the very top of the Chesil Beach somewhere back of the Fleet, snatched as it were out of the jaws of death by the hand of God? What a thing to have been present at the first telling of that incredible story, of how at one moment each sailor would have given everything his sea-chest contained for 'an acre of barren ground, long heath, brown furze', and at the next, at a single clap, of how they had been carried, ship and all, upon the back of a mountain-high wave, to be tumbled out upon the natural breakwater saddle as merry as mice in malt, with no more fear 'to lie drowning the washing of ten tides'. How did those service-men take their deliverance, those men of August luck, who, at the very moment when the greater part of the village of Fleet was being swept away—the water of the Swannery because of an unprecedented breach made by that awful hurricane in the sea-bank, having risen over twenty feet—had found themselves free and alive, hale and hearty, in less time than it takes a man to swear or spit? Did they call for meat and a tub of smuggled liquor that they might make good cheer, after their fashion, celebrating the closest brush men ever had with death in Deadman's Bay? 'When prayers are over my lady is ready'. Or did their thoughts, recalling the Scriptural name of their auspicious vessel—*Ebenezer* (Stone of Help)—take a more serious turn, their very marrow bones grateful to the goodness of the God whom they had so often worshipped on drowsy Sundays at church at Wyke or Weymouth?

In my little volume of *Dorset Essays* there is to be seen a photograph of a group of Portlanders taken by Mr Wyndham Goodden, and in these dangerous times I like well to look at the honest, honourable faces of the men that appear in it, the free faces of a folk not to be easily budged, bold fellows equally at home in the handling of a quarry crowbar as at the rowing of a long oar when all is at odds in a rough sea; men mindful of the island's traditions, with little liking for foreigners, and no kind of aptitude for the bending of the knee or the bowing of the head before the brute and boisterous force of violent men 'hardy and industrious to support tyrannic power'.

One of a Thousand

I was walking under the high sea-cliffs of Dorset, along a deserted beach. It was one of those days in early March when Nature appears suddenly, unexpectedly, aware of the approach of spring. The gulls were crying to each other far up in the clear sky. The waves were playing against the shore, like lambs at the edge of a wide meadow. All was joy.

As I walked over the idle pebbles, gleaming in the morning air, it seemed hardly credible that man, or bird, or beast, or flower, could ever die. The grim, ever-present fact of death, so sombre, so inert, appeared suddenly to have been lifted from the tender earth, to have become an airy nothing, light as the spindrift on the bright limpet-encrusted rocks. Yet deep in my heart I still knew that death did exist, that the consciousness of the dog-violet on the downs, of the green periwinkle in its pool, of the black cormorant flying with outstretched neck towards its favourite haunt, of the ploughman by the charred embers of his lunch-time fire, was in each but the veriest fragment of illuminated time between two vast vistas of silence; and right well did my living soul recoil from the ancient antagonist of earth, ejecting the thought from my mind, as I went on my way under the high chalk pillars, still arrogant, still obdurate, still unreconciled.

Suddenly my attention was arrested by an object that was trying to conceal itself in the cleft between two rocks. I went to the place, and bending down discovered that what I had seen was a bird, a sea-bird, huddled up in the dark shelter of its sunless retreat. I took it into my hands and immediately it began giving utterance to a succession of croaks, of croaks not unlike those of a raven when in mid-air it turns suddenly on its back to withstand, as best it may, the terrible darting onslaught of a peregrine falcon, falling upon it from above like a javelin. It was not long before I understood its plight; my hands had become soiled with that vile oil which modern ships spew out into the pure water of the sea. For a long time I had been aware of the cruel effect that this senseless contamination has upon the wild-fowl of the sea. Each year thousands upon thousands of birds are condemned by its means to the misery of a protracted death by starvation, the delicately contrived filaments of their feathers becoming hopelessly clogged with a substance as foul as it is insoluble.

The pitiable case of this particular bird appealed to me. Its breast feathers were solidly pasted to its famished body. Its wings were as useless to it as the wings of a penguin. Its tail was a congealed projection of gross blackness. Only its eyes were unaffected—those clear round eyes that were accustomed to receive upon their retina nothing but the curved shapes of the waves and clouds. When I wrapped it in my handkerchief its body adhered to the linen as though it had been the body of some sacred Egyptian hawk, covered with a preparation of black gum in provision for a sleep of three thousand years.

Determined, if it were possible, to intervene on its behalf, I carried it back to my coast-guard's cottage on the top of the cliff, and there with a scrubbing brush and paraffin oil endeavoured to cleanse its plumage. I was only partially successful. When I let it go after its first bath it managed to flap itself forward on its black webbed feet, but it was still unable to fly. Would I ever be able, I wondered, to renew the miracle of its nature and render its material body once more buoyant? I kept it in a small yard and fed it with strips of bacon. And what vitality it still retained, this little dishonoured bird, the contact of whose feathers was able to transform even the green grass to patches of gleaming filth! When it splashed in the bucket I could feel its body taut with electric life, taut as the body of a freshly taken trout.

Two days later it was necessary for me to go to Dorchester. I returned late in the evening, with a bagfull of smelts. It was one of those evenings of forlorn melancholy familiar enough to people who spend the winter in lonely isolated houses overlooking the sea. The grey rain was sweeping across the downs, drifting over the stunted thorn trees in white clouds, like the vanguard of a ghost army in panic-stricken retreat from some unprecedented disaster. The sound of waves breaking on the pebbles far down under the White Nore rose into the chilled air with a monotony persistent and dolorous.

It was dark when I took one of the fish to the bird, and I carried a lantern in my hand. All the melancholy of that melancholy evening seemed to have become concentrated in the little cement yard. I found the bird pressed up against one of the walls near where the water from the broken shoot was falling. I dangled the fish over the transverse grooves of its curious upper mandible. It held its head erect and looked at me with an expression at once proud and indifferent. The rain was drenching down upon me and upon my lantern, yet I caught that look and resolved the very next morning to carry it back to the sea-weed littered beach where I had found it. Better, I thought, for it to have its eyes pecked out by the herring gulls than that it should be subjected to so ignominious an imprisonment.

And all the time, had I but known it, this sea bird, this razorbill, was planning for its own release. Nature, the great mother, taught it that there still remained one gate through which it might pass unimpeded. Never again was it destined to congregate with the foolish guillemots on the higher ledges of Bats Head, never again would it deposit its single egg on those dizzy, marble-white platforms near where the samphire grows. With unbroken spirit it had summoned to its assistance the universal enemy, the universal deliverer of us all. In its extremity, this wild creature had sent out an ultimate call, and when I came to it in the morning it lay on its side in a little pool of rain-drenched oil, dead.

A Downland Burden

How beautiful is a winter's dawn on an upland downland! Often in wild weather the rising sun streaks with scarlet the clouds behind the well-laid black boughs of a thorn hedge till they suggest the red glow of a kitchen fire against the bars of a grate. But long before such a sight is to be observed the gulls have come in from the sea for their winter diet of worms, appearing as it grows lighter and lighter, like fine white china birds placed on a grass green cloth. With greedy impatience they hurry this way and that over the chill rain-drenched turf, their webbed feet serving them well for these impetuous responses to the almost inaudible rustlings of their lowly game. They come to their selected feeding places long before the night is over, their outlawed scavenging cries suddenly shattering the august stillness of the solemn valleys.

Yesterday in the dark of dawn a flock of such herring gulls was disturbed by the figure of a man. He came heavily burdened with the rabbits he had been picking up from his traps. The little animals, happily dead at last after their night of agony and terror, swayed head-downwards from a stout hedge stick. I watched him pass in the dim light and I fell to meditating on the kinds of burdens that generation after generation have been carried over these lonely hills—burdens for the most that have had to do with the labours of pastoral life, bundles of hurdle sticks, or living new-born lambs with their mothers following anxiously behind a trudging wind-blown shepherd. Our post mistress at East Chaldon, an autocratic old woman of eighty, tells how her husband sixty years ago came carrying to her cottage a May swarm all along the ridge of the downs from Church Knowl, the bees swinging in a pillow case 'at the end of his Plymouth cloak', as in those days they used to call a sturdy cudgel.

And even I in my time have carried poetical loads. After the Great War I got leave from Farmer Angus Scutt to put up an open air revolving shelter on the top of Jordan Hill, eastward of Weymouth. This historical hill has now been built over, but in those days a long row of old-fashioned coastguard cottages were the only habitable buildings to trouble the seclusion and peace of the fields. The hill had not always been so lonely. Thomas Hardy once told me that the Romans had used to dig in it for their potter's clay. They certainly lived on it for the remains of their villas have been discovered, together with a Temple to Aesculapius. A ruined cottage for years stood on the summit of this hill and it was in the garden of this cottage that I had my shelter placed. The plot was surrounded by one of those low grey walls common to the neighbourhood. In one of its corners was the old well and in another a hawthorn tree that had been scourged into a grotesque shape by I know not how many rushing gales blowing across from the Chesil Beach. On an autumn day the enclosure could appear desolate enough with the individual pennant leaves of the nettles flapping to and fro in the drifting rain. On summer afternoons, however, the hot overgrown grass-entangled seaside garth would seem to hold even yet its lost memories, so that I could almost hear the splash of the bucket as it struck the well water, and almost see the daughter of the house return to the whitewashed kitchen, one white bare arm holding the handle of her dipper. All day long butterflies would flit from one flower head to another in the unkempt bland enclosure, till this tiny parcel of ground would appear utterly given over to old remembrance of the past and the delicate delight of the coloured insects in the summer sunshine of the present.

I was walking back to Weymouth from my retreat one November

afternoon when I noticed that the fishermen were dragging their nets onto the beach that lies opposite to the marshland named Lodmoor. A draught of fishes being drawn out of the sea has never failed to arouse my imagination. An alien population of shining, voiceless creatures leaping for freedom, leaping for life in the meshes of a rough treacherous web corked and smelling of tar. I bought half a dozen herring.

That night what wind there was swung round to the north east and every bent grass in the lonely garden was ridged with a rime of frost, each particle clear to be seen in the bright moonlight. The idea then suddenly came to me that I would carry my herrings in the early hours of the morning over the downs to East Chaldon and surprise my brother Theodore. I left Jordan Hill at half-past three, and in unlucky hours I have often solaced myself by recalling the extraordinary revelation I received from this walk, especially from the sleeping village of Preston as I passed through it. A little beyond the old Roman bridge, perhaps half way up the street, I stood still. The air was cold, the road hard and twisted, and the stars bright beyond conception. I waited. I could hear no sound except the steady ticking of a clock in the nearest cottage. Bird and beast and man, all were sleeping. No cares now vexed the minds of the old men and old women, no fears or disappointments vexed the heads of the children of the village. All was forgotten and cancelled, the anxieties of the clergyman in his ivied vicarage, of the sailor boy, of the ploughman, of the butcher and the publican, the worries of the servant girl who a few hours before was lightly laughing behind a privet hedge. This ancient Dorset village seemed lying in an absolute silence at the heart of a crystal sphere like a mediaeval village whose energetic clatter had been by some Merlin-craft strangely suspended for the nonce, but whose feckless, foolish riot would presently be once more free of the spell. These dreamers, who lay so whist under tile and thatch had, without thought or intention, attained to a state half-way approximating that of the dumb host close-closeted in the key-hole churchyard overlooking a valley where an inland rushy stream, innocent of its fate, slowly wound its way towards the suck and ebb of sea waves. In these small, low ancient chambers of births, of love-makings and of deaths, chambers smelling of apples kept in drawers, and stuffy quilts—were there perhaps other beings besides those that breathed, revenants irresistibly drawn back, with finger on lip, to the darker local corners of the house never reached by moonlight? Tick tock, tick tock. Long after I had left behind me The Plough Inn that stood on Preston Hill my mind retained this reassuring echo by which man, lost in an abyss of eternity, audaciously contrives to tally off, and render reasonable the flickering, miraculous moments he is spending in the blind firmament of nature.

Leaving the road at Poxwell I came upon the lonely stretch of downs that leads through Holworth to Chaldon. When I reached the stone circle I rested. The fish were still wrapped about in the shell of newspaper the fishermen had given me, but in walking the paper had become damp. Cleansing them as best I could of the adhering scraps of moist print I laid them out in the row upon the hoar frost. The stones of the Poxwell circle stood scarcely more than a foot or so out of the ground. And yet unobtrusive as they are it is impressive to consider that they were rolled here by Neolithic man, celebrants of fertility, worshippers of the sun. And what liberal breaths my being seemed to take under the cold clear sky of the first hard frost of the year! Sometimes as I walked over the stiff grass I would see the white scut of a rabbit fast disappearing between the tough tussocks left uneaten by the grazing cattle. The holly trees against the grey wall, used to being rifled by their berries during the week before Christmas, held up their dark leaves bright as metal in the moonlight. My way led me close by the old farm at West Chaldon and as I came through the yard I noticed a light in one of the windows. It shone warm and yellow, and the glow of the candle of this little early morning servant glittering beneath the Dorset thatch has never by me been forgotten, so friendly did the first stir of life seem after that journey, and poetical too in its suggestion of cockroach wintry warmth-retaining early morning kitchens with the dawn appearing gradually paler and paler.

In Stevenson's story 'Will O' the Mill', a stranger visits the wise miller as he meditates in his summer garden, odorous with the scent of heliotropes. The stranger is none other than John Death, and presently he taps the arm of his genial, philosophic host with the significant words—'The Time has come'. As soon as I reached my brother's house I stood in the moonlight outside his bedroom and in as horrid a voice as I could I uttered these same words, for in those days we were both firm and hearty and there was no impropriety in such japes.

In a moment my sister-in-law, always blithely responsive to such unexpected events, had opened the door—and what a breakfast she prepared, and how merry and mellow my brother was, and how his two little boys made me describe my walk urging me again and again to imitate the barking of the fox I had heard coming through the Holworth Valley. Nor did they forget to ask whether there were plenty of berries on the holly trees. And my spirits were not less high than theirs, and always I held at the back of my mind to remember like a talisman against all future invasions of the commonplace the sight of the six deep-sea herrings I had carried, lying in a row in the centre of the old stone circle, their plump sides in the moonlight more glittering than the frost.

Recollections of Thomas Hardy

In the spring of 1938 there was an auction sale at Max Gate of all the possessions of Thomas Hardy that had not been judged of sufficient interest to be included amongst the objects bequeathed by Mrs Hardy to the County Museum at Dorchester. A report of the sale appeared in the local paper and to one who has for many years known and honoured Mr Hardy the account given of the final dispersal of his goods could not fail to be moving. 'The Three Marys', a small picture that had once been in the possession of Thomas Hardy's neighbour, William Barnes, fetched no more than four-and-a-half guineas, and this in spite of the fact that it bore the inscription in the novelist's handwriting 'bought at sale of Wm. Barnes Dorset poet, by Tho. Hardy'. Came Rectory, where William Barnes spent the evening of his life, stands scarcely half a mile distant from Max Gate.

It was reported that a walking stick of Hardy's was knocked down to a Dorset farmer for twelve shillings, and that the looking-glass from his bedroom, for a sum no more considerable, fell to the bidding of an unknown young lady. We can scarcely doubt that the two last auction chances would have pleased the poet. In what better hands could his staff have fallen than in those of a man all the hours of whose life would be spent in the hayfields, harvest fields, stables, cow-yards, and marketplaces of Wessex? And how could 'casualty' have indulged Hardy's fancy more than to have placed his familiar dressing-table mirror in the possession of so enterprising a bargainer? On how many mornings of neutral tone had not this crystal plate reflected the countenance of 'a thinker of crooked thoughts upon Life in the sere!' It would do so now no longer. In its place the bright features of a young girl would shine out in the bedroom light, with cool hands arranging her hair, while planning perhaps for a summer tryst in a Frome valley buttercup meadow, or in some well-selected bracken hollow of Bockhampton heath.

This plain newspaper report of the sale at Max Gate set me pondering on Hardy's long life and especially upon those occasions when I myself had been privileged to be in his presence.

The house of his birth still stands at the furthest end of Upper Bockhampton's blind lane and I do not think any great man ever had a nativity home more suited to his genius than is this small unobtrusive Dorset freeehold cottage, with its thatched roof embowered among the apple trees of its own small garden, to that of Thomas Hardy. Over the hedge of the plot, on both sides of the lane, great forest trees tower high, huge-boughed leafy trees in which all day long rooks caw, wood-pigeons murmur, and small birds twitter and sing and flutter from one cool shadow to another. On the further side of the white gate which marks the end of this sequestered privet-hedge-way lies the great heath of *The Return of the Native* with its acres of fern and heather. It was here that Hardy played as a child and it was here that he experienced his first passionate love affair. In such a locality it would be strange indeed if the mind of a young man had not turned to thoughts of love. Nowhere in Dorset do primroses cluster more gently about the beech tree boles; nowhere in Dorset do the silver rains of a midsummer morning patter more softly down through the woodland foliage; nowhere in Dorset can there be found safer and more secret 'lover's cabinets' than amongst the tall stiff-turreted bracken jungles of this wild, west country heath.

Mr Middleton Murry told me once that Hardy's first memory was of looking at the shining belly of a kitchen kettle brought from

Dorchester market by his mother who in the very heart of Victoria's spacious reign had fallen in love with Mr Hardy's father, the black-bearded village builder, her maidenly heart being struck, in an instant, by the mere spectacle of an elbow wagging at an old viol up in the musician's gallery of Stinsford church. The kitchen utensil was truly an honourable and a fitting first memory for a great poet, a memory Homeric in its association with man's common needs on earth where receptacles of clay, of bronze, of copper, or of iron have for so many millennia been used for convenience in eating and drinking.

It was in the nineties, I think, that I first heard the syllables of Thomas Hardy's name spoken. We had all been invited to the Abbey at Montacute for a picnic and there was present at the gathering the West Country novelist Walter Raymond. It was this man, with his fine head of white hair, who informed my brother John in a spirit of modesty as charming as it was magnanimous that there was living in Dorset a writer far greater than himself. When a few years later my brother's first volume of youthful poems was published it contained an Ode addressed to Hardy:

> Master of human smiles and human moan,
> Of strange soul-searchings, raptures, agonies,
> Passions that ask for bread and find a stone,
> Hopes hungered into madness like the seas,
> And pity dumb with pleading like the wind:
> Prophet art thou of that mysterious tongue
> Wherewith our ancient Mother, deaf and blind,
> Her griefs immortal and her joys hath sung
> In the unheeding ears of human-kind.
> ...
> And there, in commune with thy mighty heart,
> I saw how life's light wreath of summer roses
> Remorseless Fate's inveterate frown discloses,
> And sullen Death's intolerable dart:
> Saw man's last hope beneath a soulless sky,
> To live for Love, and for Love's sake to die.

The novelist was obviously gratified and wrote an encouraging letter, a courtesy which later resulted in my brother paying a visit to Max Gate. Hardy did not fail to appreciate John Cowper's temperament, with its romantic undisciplined imaginings. The friendship between the two men, and Mr Hardy's confidence in my brother's remarkable gifts, lasted until the novelist's death.

I well remember my brother's return from his first visit to Max Gate. It was during the summer holidays, and the rest of us children were crowded together in a wooden hut which my youngest brother had built for himself in one of the shrubberies. This brother had invited us all to tea and his saucepan was just beginning to boil under the laurel bushes when John appeared full of exciting talk about his expedition. I recollect how he drew for us a caricature of Hardy on one of the white deal boards that formed the walls of this 'Bushes' home', a striking picture of the novelist that the passages of snail, ant, and wood-louse were never able quite to obliterate. Especially did the sketch emphasise the writer's hooked nose and goblin eyebrows. It was, I believe, in these same holidays that Hardy and his first wife paid us a visit. They walked up from the station at Montacute arriving at the Vicarage in time for luncheon. Hardy, I remember, wore a pair of tight snuff-coloured trousers which oddly contrasted with the more sober colour of the upper part of his dress. My father had not read a word he had ever written, but he had heard rumours enough of the freedom of his thought to qualify his enthusiasm for this new hero that his eldest son had discovered. My mother's attitude was different. Her literary interests had always been so strong that any writer would have been honoured by her, and, as Mr Hardy's place was at her right hand, all went well. Hardy at the time must have been about fifty years old. His lips were pale and his face did not give the impression of good health and I remember my mother rashly predicted that he would not live to a great age. The first Mrs Hardy was a kindly woman whose forehead was adorned by two curls which appeared to my irreverent little boy's fancy like the feathers at the end of a drake's tail.

In the afternoon my brother took Mr Hardy over Montacute House and through the village, finally returning to the Vicarage in time for him to write in the visitor's book of the 'Mabelulu', another garden play house that my brother Bertie and my sister May and I had built, the words—*Thomas Hardy. A Wayfarer*. After the old-fashioned family tea was at an end John and my sister Gertrude and I accompanied our guests to the country station. It was a lovely summer's evening and presently I found myself sitting alone with Hardy on the well-varnished yellow-painted bench that was on the platform outside the lamp room. He remained silent with his legs crossed as though absorbed in contemplation of the quiet landscape. Suddenly it came into my head to begin to describe to him the dancing that each summer took place on the Club Day and at the School Treat under the village apple trees. I told him how these dances would continue late into the night, which was to say the least of it a gross exaggeration, for my father would soon grow uneasy if ever the Kingsbury band continued to play by the lee light of the moon; and in my eager eloquence I referred to the remarkable number of old-world dances that still were known in the district. I had intended that this second prevarication should arouse the poet's attention but I was not at all prepared for the extreme interest that he now showed, as, concentrating his whole mind upon me, he began asking for the names of these same dances, prosecuting his enquiries with a resolution not easy to be evaded even when my brother came to join us. The mortification I felt as I sat on that bench in my white flannel trousers, green at the knees from where I had recently fallen, has remained with me to this day, together with a clear memory of those suspended moments before the train's arrival, with voices of harvesters coming from a distant field and the look of the softness of the summer grass opposite, where cows moved at peace under a mackerel sky.

The next time I saw Hardy was after I had come down from Cambridge. I had been staying with my brother Theodore at East Chaldon. This little village is situated some ten miles from Max Gate, and I ventured on my way home as I had two hours to wait in Dorchester, to call. I was extremely nervous as I approached the front door by the short curving drive. The servant showed me into the drawing-room. I observed the room narrowly. There was a bust of Sir Walter Scott at the top of a tall book case and, on each side of the fireplace, pictures of Shelley and of John Keats. I also noticed a small water-colour of Westminster Abbey painted by Hardy himself when he was a young man. Mrs Hardy presently entered the room. She informed me that she had sent a servant up to Mr Hardy's study but doubted whether he would be able to come down and see me. She was mistaken, however, for almost immediately the door opened and Mr Hardy himself entered looking to me unchanged from what he had been on the occasion of his visit to Montacute. He asked me questions about Chaldon and also talked to me about my future plans. I remember he advised me to join the Dorset Society in London. My romantic hero-worship could scarcely be concealed. He must have seen it shining out of my eyes. I did not dare to stay long and when I rose to leave he conducted me to the garden gate, truly a signal courtesy to offer so excitable and immature a youth. Before taking my leave I ventured to ask him what he was then writing, and well do I remember his answering with a kindly, self-deprecatory, quizzical glance that he was occupied with *The Dynasts*.

I walked away in an ecstasy at having once more seen him and I remember buying a picture postcard in Dorchester, which not only included a drawing of Hardy's head, but also a miniature sketch of the novelist's home. This postcard I had the temerity to send to H. R. King, my old school master at Sherborne, telling him that I had just returned from a visit to 'the greatest living English writer', words that must have appeared grandiloquent enough to the sarcastic, lovable, old pedant to whom they were addressed, a man whose fad it was to believe that English literature had reached its glome with Wordsworth, Dickens and Thackeray. *The Dynasts* is an epic I have always admired greatly, but apparently such appreciation has not been universal. Edward Clodd once told my friend Louis Wilkinson that on his stepping to his bookshelf on the occasion of a visit of Meredith to Aldburgh, the novelist's cold, cultivated, sarcastic voice had sounded across the lamp-lit summer room 'I hope you are not bringing us *The Dynasts*'. At the time of which I write George Meredith was still considered in the know-all contemporary literary world of far more consequence than Hardy and it has been a deep satisfaction to me that I lived long enough to see so shallow a judgement reversed and the native, homespun, Shakespearean genius of Hardy reverenced above the fashionable clever talent of the mannered stylist of whom Scawen Blunt remarked 'tailoring parentage was the great tragedy of Meredith's life'. An interesting contrast between the essential natures of the two men is afforded by the following odd happening. When Wilde was serving time in Reading Gaol a movement was started to petition the Home Secretary for the shortening of his sentence. Overtures were made to the leading men-of-letters to see how many of them would be willing to give support to such a project. Hardy volunteered at once to sign the paper, but Meredith, sensitive to the popular feeling which had been aroused, refused to have anything to do with it. And yet Oscar Wilde and his manners were extraordinarily remote from the simplicities of Hardy's upbringing and character. 'Is not Oscar Wilde rather a hard-hearted man?' he once said to my brother John.

At this period I spent a year or more at Davos Platz and on my return to England my brother Theodore invited me to stay with him at Chaldon. It was during the summer of 1911 and this should have given me a good opportunity of other visits to Max Gate. Such a possibility however was upset by the following childish incident. One of my sisters was an enthusiastic collector of autographs and as she was passing Max Gate one day on her bicycle it occurred to her that Hardy's signature would make a notable addition to her book. She did not know that it was Hardy's custom never to indulge such requests. Her discomfiture was only matched by my own consternation when she confided her unlucky adventure to me with the words, 'Well, I don't think much of your great hero.' The embarrassment I underwent over the solecism tormented my foolish mind so much that I never ventured to make a single overture in the direction of Max Gate during the whole time I was staying with my brother. I did not, however, abandon the vain hope that either in the streets of Weymouth or of Dorchester I might one day meet Mr Hardy by chance face to face.

One evening, when sheltering in the waiting-room of the little wayside station of Moreton before starting for my dark walk across the moor to Chaldon, I imagined for a few moments that my sanguine expectations had actually been fulfilled. Just as I was about to set out the London express came in. In a brightly-lighted first class carriage opposite where I stood I was sure that I recognised the familiar features of the novelist. The drenching rain that ceaselessly splashed down upon the roofless lamplit platform made it difficult for me to see clearly and for several minutes I remained motionless gazing and gazing through the carriage window dimmed to a mysterious opaqueness by the continual stream of rain drops. Presently the traveller who was, in actual fact, a perfect stranger noticed the exaggerated attention I was giving him and to my utter confusion I received in response to my stare of childish adoration the patronizing easy smile of an unpleasantly supercilious First Class passenger.

In the early spring of the following year I was again in Switzerland.

It was on my return from this second convalescence in the Alps that I began to try to write. My first paper was entitled 'Death' and in later years it was included in an early collection of essays called *Ebony and Ivory*. I sent the article to the *New Age* and immediately received an answer in Mr Orage's artistic, spider-like writing accepting it and assuring me that it was 'good enough for publication in any journal'. No eaglet who for the first time tries the strength of its wings could have been prouder than I was on reading his words, and, as soon as the piece was printed I ordered several copies of the weekly, one of which I ventured to post to Max Gate. An answer came back by return from Mr Hardy thanking me for my kindness and saying he had enjoyed reading my article very much indeed, adding that he himself had but recently passed through just such an experience as I described. There is no doubt that Mr Hardy had felt the death of his first wife—the heroine of *A Pair of Blue Eyes*—deeply.

With the greatest pride I showed the letter to my brother John and I well remember his declaring that only a really great man would ever have been willing to write in so intimate and natural a way to a young writer who had nothing but enthusiasm to commend him.

In the year 1919, after an exile in Africa of five years, I was again back in England. My father by that time had resigned the living of Montacute and had retired to Weymouth so that once more I found myself in easy reach of Mr Hardy. My sister Gertrude arranged that I should go to tea one afternoon at Max Gate. I reached Dorchester in plenty of time and crossing the railway bridge slowly approached the house. The young chestnuts that bordered the road were in fresh leaf and although I was now thirty-five years old, my heart seemed no less responsive, no less romantic than on the occasion of my former visit. And yet I was discouraged also. My African sojourn had interrupted my writing career and I could not catch the attention of a single editor. At the back of my mind I held to the hope that Hardy would be able to give me just the advice I wanted. All turned out different. He was no longer the grave-eyed man-of-letters I had remembered. My impression as he crossed the small hall to shake hands with me remains fixed in my mind. He was dressed in a tweed suit that might have belonged to any country squire, a suit that seemed to suggest partridge-shooting, with calls of 'mark over', rather than the quiet of a writer's study. It was as if old age had not only lightened his marrow bones but gone a little to his head. I realized at once that the hope I had entertained of getting help from this talkative, dapper little gentleman was an empty one, and sitting at tea I contented myself with listening respectfully to his anecdotal memories of old Dorchester.

In my desire to make some kind of impression I would sometimes relate my own sensational experiences in Africa. The diffidence I felt in approaching the subject of my personal affairs was increased by the fact that I was not the only guest. When I was first shown into the drawing room I had found myself in the company of a young woman occupied in playing with a white terrier. This terrier was the dog name Wessex who held an important place in the last years of Hardy's life. The young lady diverted herself with the animal in a way that showed her as being a familiar and favoured visitor and I received the same impression when her husband arrived, a self-possessed young man who wrote reviews, so I was told afterward, for the *Times Literary Supplement*. I myself had only written for the *New Age* yet this young scholar from London and Oxford, living at a nearby mill (which of the mills I never discovered) had already at twenty-five firmly established himself in contemporary literary circles. The two young people left after tea and while Mr Hardy was conducting them to the garden gate I stood with Mrs Hardy at the window. We looked out at the spring twilight in silence. It was the first time that I had met Mr Hardy's second wife. She was a dark, nervous woman of an awkward carriage, but one who possessed an odd distinction of her own. As I stood by her side in that room emptied of its company I received a draught of romantic Bronte-like melancholy the strength of which I have never forgotten. In after years Mrs Hardy, on more than one occasion, proved herself a good friend to me, but I never rid myself altogether of that first impression of a hopeless attitude of life-disavowal which seemed, indeed, to find ultimate justification in her lingering death from a malignant cancer in middle life. At tea I had ventured to speak of an essay I was writing on the engraver Bewick, and I remember Mr Hardy referring to one of the famous tail-pieces that represented the old North Countryman's own coffin being carried away from his home, Cherryburn, a house of stone very bleak in appearance, so Hardy explained.

Six years passed before I saw Mr Hardy again. I had been living during this time in New York City. Though I found it difficult to earn my living by writing these were happy years, and in due time under the wise and understanding guidance of Mr Alfred Harcourt America gradually began to give me the recognition that I had failed to win in England. The necessity of paying the monthly rent of my hall-bedroom (into which the sun only shone by reflection from the factory opposite) often put me to my shifts and on the occasion of one of these crises the idea came to me of writing an article on Thomas Hardy for *The Dial*. In this article I was indiscreet enough to allude to a conversation I had had with him which seemed to be of general literary interest. He had confided to me, as we sat talking together after tea, that he remembered as a boy a family of saddlers living in the nearby village of Broadmayne named Keats and, recalling that John Keats's forebears had been saddlers, he had often wondered whether this Dorset family could not have been related to the poet, a surmise that appeared to receive a support from the fact that the features of some of the members of the Broadmayne saddlering family had, he had often thought, remarkable racial resemblance to those of the author of *Endymion*. Indeed he told me that he had sometimes indulged his fancy that Keats might have actually walked over the downs to visit these West Country cousins during those days when, on his voyage to Rome, his ship, because of bad weather, was driven to take shelter in Lulworth Cove, where was composed the famous last sonnet, with thoughts of hills, stars and the sea, unmistakeably reminiscent of this particular Dorset locality landscape.

As ill-luck would have it my essay fell under the all-seeing eye of Amy Lowell who was just then collecting material for her biography of Keats—and what must she do but bustle off to Max Gate to harass Mr Hardy with cross-questionings after the manner of one who wants facts rather than fiction and has a mind to sift all evidence to the bottom! It was not until I had returned once more to Dorset with my American wife, Miss Gregory, that the full repercussion of this awkward affair reached me. My brother John, as was his custom, had written to ask whether he could pay his summer visit to Max Gate and on this occasion bring with him my brother Theodore. Just before the two of them left East Chaldon a letter arrived from Mrs Hardy complaining of my ill-conduct in having published in *The Dial* an intimate communication that had never been intended for literary use. My brother Theodore, though he had already put on his Sunday jacket, forthwith abandoned out of hand all idea of visiting Max Gate, and as those who know him will guess, much Frome water had to flow under Gray's Bridge before ever he crossed the great man's threshold. I felt humiliated on my own account, and indignant with Miss Lowell, recalling with renewed irritation the bluntness of her speech when, on our first being introduced, she had remarked in her autocratic manner 'in any case I am glad you are not your brother'.

The vexing business was not quickly forgotten. I was truly concerned that I had given Mr Hardy this trouble and I wrote the most propitiatory letters to Mrs Hardy. Eventually the notion came into my head to send Mr Hardy a snake's skin for a book marker. The skin I had taken from an adder I myself had killed in the long cliff grass. I think it was this homely tribute from the White Nose that finally caused him to forget his annoyance. He even made an attempt to call on us in our coastguard cottage, but found the exertion of walking so far over the open downs too much for his octogenarian bones. It was at this time that I received a letter from Mr Clarence Darrow, the American lawyer, who was on a visit to England, asking whether I could arrange a meeting for him with Thomas Hardy. Under the circumstances it was not an easy piece of diplomacy, but when it had been arranged and the two famous men did meet, all went well.

Not long after Mrs Hardy invited Miss Gregory and me to tea at Max Gate. The visit remains one of my happiest memories. In his great old age Mr Hardy had recovered the simplicity and dignity so native to his genius. When I left his presence I felt as I might have done had I been sheltering behind an old hedgerow holly, or under the wall of an ancient grange, or with back against a grey-wether on Salisbury Plain. He appeared to have forgiven and forgotten all about the Amy Lowell worry. We talked together freely on many matters. He insisted that the correct name for the cliff on which we lived was White Nose and not White Nore or White Nothe, all of which names are to be read upon maps. 'The name of the cliff is White Nose and if you stand and look at it from Weymouth esplanade the reason for its being so named becomes clear. It is like a human nose, like Wellington's nose.' He was particularly anxious to learn, and it was so characteristic of his mind, deep sinking always to the simplest facts of life, how we managed to get on for water in so remote a place. I explained that the government had built large cisterns for the storing of the rain water from the roofs.

The idea pleased him and he declared that rain water was more wholesome for drinking purposes than spring water. Horses, he said, will always choose the water of the foulest pond that has had sun and air upon it rather than that of the purest fountains that jet up from the earth. 'Water that has stood a while is good for the "Bots",' the old man concluded.

We mentioned, I remember, Frank Harris. I told him that I had been reading his *The Man Shakespeare* and found the book penetrating in certain ways though I was repelled by its lack of style. How could he, for example, use the objectionable word 'smutty' in connection with Ophelia? Hardy sympathized with this resentment. He concluded the subject by remarking that Frank Harris had the gruffest voice of any man he had ever heard speak, an observation with which I could acquiesce, well remembering how Harris, after having driven me back to my Waverly Place lodgings, had boomed out at the top of his voice so that the whole street might have heard him: 'It will all come out in the wash'—a remark that referred to the approaching publication of his *My Life and Loves*. Hardy spoke also of the degrading influence of blood sports and told me that he believed that the feeling of the general public towards animals was far more sensitive than it had been in his childhood. Even on the farm the labourers were now not so brutal. He recalled as a young man remonstrating with a carter for flogging his mare and receiving the answer 'But she bain't no Christian', a remark that suggested to my mind an odd expression of the Alpine graziers—the utterance *unzanimegezellt* that must invariably accompany every reference to the cattle that these hardy stockmen spend their lives in tending, and which, literally, means 'not to be confused with men'—an utterance coming without doubt into use as a cabala to emphasize this same sense of the 'pathos of difference' which the religious have always believed to exist between man and the beast who has no soul.

I remember telling him that a pair of ravens was still to be seen frequenting the precipitous walls of our great sea promontory. In his boyhood he said these birds were much more common and he had often observed cottage people bless themselves on seeing one of the dolorous fowls fly over their 'tuns' (chimneys) in the village of Bockhampton.

When we rose to leave he walked with us to his white garden gate and it was here that I said good-bye to him for the last time. News of his death reached me when I was in New York as visiting literary critic for the *Herald Tribune* in the winter of 1928.

When I returned to England Mrs Hardy invited us to stay at Max Gate and I slept in Mr Hardy's dressing room. There hung over my head an old oil painting of a shepherd. I could scarcely imagine a portrait more in harmony with Hardy's own much-enduring genius than was this weathered countenance of the herdsman under a felt hat. Here was a man who must have hurdled many a flock of ewes, a man whose thumbs must often have been greasy from handling of fells. The picture pleased me extremely and Mrs Hardy told me it was one of which Mr Hardy himself was particularly fond. He had bought it in Salisbury. It was necessary for me to leave England for Switzerland soon afterwards and I never saw Mrs Hardy again. On receiving, in my exile, the local paper with the account of the Max Gate sale I wrote to the auctioneer asking whether this picture of the shepherd had been sold. He remembered it well, and it had been sold, but he promised if possible to trace it for me. Homer is fond of using the words 'Shepherd of the people' for the Heroes he sings of. Such a shepherd Hardy surely was. No one since Shakespeare has understood so well the troubled hearts of human beings and especially of women. But his comprehensive compassion reached to the dumb beasts—to the cattle penned for butchering, to the pheasants preserved for slaughtering, even to the humble hedgehogs that crossed the dewy lawns of Max Gate on summer nights. How fitting, how full of his own simple inspirations was the poem he wrote anticipating his death:

> When the Present has latched its postern behind my
>   tremulous stay,
> And the May month flaps its glad green leaves like wings,
> Delicate filmed as new-spun silk, will the neighbours say,
> 'He was a man who used to notice such things'?

Hedgehogs

There are certain animals that have never failed to astonish human beings by their uncouth, original and unexpected shapes. Pre-eminent among these prodigies of the earth's fair field are the 'giddy flitter mice with leather wings'. The imagination of the most clownish country boy will give instant response to the sight of a bat, dead on a granary floor. He will take it up to examine it closely, this bread-crumb wainscot-mouse whose explicit anatomy has been provided with membrane wings to fly free over the hayfields, mocking the dull ears of mortals with the shrill screams of its goblin world.

Of creatures ordained to creep over the face of the earth in England the hedgehog may be chosen first on the list for strangeness of being. How in truth could it fail to be a gazing stock, an object of wonder, this odd animal that moves across the ground encased in so invulnerable a surcoat of criss-cross prickles? From the earliest times hedgehogs have been associated with the occult. Elves, it used to be thought, were fond of 'entering into' the sturdy bodies of hedgehogs, regarding their squat, invincible forms in the light of favourable habitations, after the same manner that the devils of Galilee became incarnate in the unhallowed corporeal flesh of the Gadarene swine. Perhaps it is the great antiquity of the hedgehog race that accounts for many of its eldritch characteristics. It is reported to be one of the oldest genera of mammals. Its bones have been found unchanged from their present shape in deposits dating from the Miocene period; and that it actually does possess startling innate properties of constitution may be deduced from its singular immunity from so deadly a poison as prussic acid, hedgehogs having been known to grow plump on a diet of this condiment.

Thomas Fuller in his *Worthies of England* says that 'this animal which carries a stand of pikes on his back' is most numerous in Hertfordshire. 'Plenty of hedgehogs are found in this woodland county. They too often suck the kine there,' and he adds in his whimsical fashion, 'though the dayry-maids conne them small thanks for sparing them pains in milking them.' Whether hedgehogs do or do not drink from the overflowing udders of dairy cows is still a disputed question, as is also the manner of their device for transfixing fallen fruit by rolling on it, a rumour that hardly seems to accord with the remarkably low and remarkably primitive brain-development that is supposed to be theirs.

> Apples, or pears, or grapes, such is his meate,
> Which on his back he carries for to eate.

In September a hedgehog was found one early morning swimming about in a small goldfish-pond in my garden. In its efforts to drink, for they are thirsty animals, it had tumbled in. It may very well have been swimming for its life for hours, its long black flexible snout held high above the water's surface as it paddled itself round between the flat waterlily leaves. With the aid of a bucket it was rescued. It was, however, chilled and exhausted, and several hours passed before it made any effort to move from where it had been left to recover itself on the grass. Then as the sun's increasing strength gradually warmed its quaint pelt it revived, and, disregarding the saucer of milk that had been placed by its head, sedately moved off in the direction of a clump of gorse bushes sheltering a row of bee-hives, seeming thereby to conform to Lyly's assertion that the hedgehog 'ever more lodgeth in the thornes because he himself is so full of prickells'.

The ceremonious retreat offered a supreme example of the proper conduct of a dignified withdrawal from the public eye. The little beast's deportment was grave but devoid of fear. It observed us with its cautious but firm brown eyes, and then with undaunted deliberation set about its stately departure.

Once long ago in Africa a Somali trader who was bringing down a herd of native cattle from the Boran called at my hut to borrow a blanket that it was my custom to place under the saddle of my mule. When the man detected my churlish loan, from having observed grey mule's hairs in the warp of the blanket, he managed to convey a rebuke in the manner of his leave-taking, even his black heels that showed from under his robe as he stalked away expressing the contempt he felt for my lack of courtesy. The recovered hedgehog made off in much the same manner. Now it displayed the black heel of its right-hand foot, now the black heel of its left-hand foot, and as if it were gathering its rough shirt about it like any hermit of the simple life it set off for the sequestered haunt of its own secret knowledge.

What romance is suggested by the mere idea of these creatures with their absorbed midnight expeditions! To think of them is to be reminded of those lovely mild evenings at the end of the summer holidays when they are most often to be met with foraging for their indiscriminate viands in quiet dew-saturated gardens where vast hosts of peace-loving snails with dextral shells, wide wet mouths, and wavering horns attend dim banquets in untroubled ease.

Those of us who have allowed our minds to be besotted by the pressure of personal affairs, who perhaps are wasting our time in amassing wealth that we can never hope to enjoy, might well have our folly corrected by an accidental glimpse of this self-contained individualist in his shirt of thorns moving out of the cavernous shadows of some cool odorous flower-bed. Through the trembling leaves of the garden trees the summer stars shine bright on the outlandish back of the small quadruped, impressing the conscious intelligence with a clear comprehension of the wealth of earth-poetry revealed by the mere existence of so fabulous an urchin directing its activities by the light of the Milky Way.

Chainey Bottom

If a traveller walks along the gypsy track leading from White Nose to Diffey's Farm above Lulworth he will notice that the downs on his right hand side fall away in steep valleys that extend to the edge of the chalk cliffs. The names locally given to these formations are West Bottom, Middle Bottom, Chainey Bottom and Scratchy Bottom. It is probable that all four of the valleys have been used at one time or another for the habitation of human beings, for they are all of them well protected from the north winds.

That Chainey Bottom was once thickly populated there can be no doubt. Unmistakeable traces of a prosperous Celtic settlement are still to be seen on the ancient chalk hills. When the sun's rays lie low upon the grass either at dawn or on a cloudless evening the downland slopes are chequered with the boundary ridges of old cultivation plots which, straight as the baulks of medieval common lands, intersect with shadows the sea-gull feathered turf.

On the side of Swyre Head they fall into geometrical figures, figures that might have been carefully traced out by a mathematical giant, though long since abandoned to a leisurely attrition from the pads of foxes, from the clawed hairy feet of rabbits, and from the unceasing festivals of the earth-worm tribe with appetites gluttonous for mud.

When I was living in one of the coastguard cottages of the White Nose Mr Salzman, the historian from Cambridge, let me have several fragments of Bronze Age pottery that he had picked up in Chainey Bottom. This courtesy once more aroused my interest in the valley and I began to examine it carefully. I had often noticed odd heaps of flints lying about in its basin. These heaps were circular in shape, and my brother, A. R. Powys, suggested that they marked the places where the more important huts of the early settlement had once stood, huts with sunken flint-paved floors, and low flint walls surmounted by roofs of wattle and thatch.

The fishermen and trappers with whom I talked always declared that the flints had been heaped together so that smuggled brandy kegs could be buried in this unfrequented valley without arousing the suspicion of custom house officers by any disturbance of surface soil. My brother's theory seemed to me the more plausible of the two. It was, I do not deny, hard to believe that it had taken more than two thousand years for a circumference so limited to be covered by the encroaching grass, but this might be explained by the fact that the flints lay very deep one upon the other in the original saucer-shaped bed of the hut and every advance made by the grass during wet autumns might well be cancelled in the summer when the hot sun would perish the roots trying to find nutriment on such stony ground.

In the summer of 1930 we obtained the permission of the late Mr Herbert Weld to excavate one of these flint circles. Mr Prideaux, the curator of Dorchester Museum, was present during the digging. The loose flints lay several feet deep and when the floor was eventually reached it was found to be cobbled in a layer of clay which must have been conveyed to Chainey Bottom from a distance.

It is strange to think how the material traces of a culture will often last on unnoticed through the centuries! How few summer visitors to Dorset have imagined, when from the top of Bat's Head, they have glanced casually down at a few scattered heaps of weather-patinated flints, that in actual fact their eyes were resting upon ruins of human dwelling places far older than those they so much admire at Corfe Castle. When once its history has been learned this wild falcon-visited, raven-haunted Bottom can be looked upon with new eyes. Each cultivated acre of its old inhabitants is plain to be seen; the winding trackways into the valley and the winding trackways out of the valley can be distinguished; the well they dug and used is visible, and taking Chainey Bottom as the clue to the district, it becomes apparent that the man-made features dominating this ancient hill country belong neither to our age nor to the medieval age, but to the Bronze Age.

On the crest of Hambury Tout is a remarkable barrow, and within the radius of a mile it would be possible to find a dozen of such ancient burying mounds. Further away to the east Ring Hill with its marvellous trenches is visible half across the county. In the middle of wide corn lands to the left of the gypsies' track stands an earthwork which on the Ordnance map is named 'The Pound'. It resembles an enormous Masai cattle boma with a diameter of perhaps thirty yards but large enough to give safe harbourage to hundreds of cows in an hour of danger.

If when I am occupied with my favourite pastime of looking for worked flints I raise my eyes from the furrow I am following on the great upland field, I see the sturdy outline of this primitive fortification unaltered from what it was when its huge banks were first piled up with stag horn picks. It is a magical earth circle, patient and strong, that binds our generation to the generation of that older time, that binds us to men and women who in their day marked with intelligence the configurations of the stars moving in stately procession across the sky of their valley which today is disturbed by but one sound—the breaking sea waves on the beach of the Durdle Door.

Worked Flints

I had been living on the Dorset downs many years before ever I thought about looking for flints chipped and worked into serviceable shapes by our Neolithic ancestors. I was under the impression that they were difficult to find, and then one day I suddenly appreciated the fact that the uplands were strewn with them. Indeed, so closely populated must the downs have been that it is impossible to walk ten yards over a ploughed field without finding one of these artefacts brought to the surface by the coulter.

It was upon these high downs with their calling lapwing, their fresh flowers and lonely wind-scourged thorns that these Stone Age men lived out their lives. To this very day the clear downland champain, of sky, sea and chalk retains evidence upon evidence of their age-long presences. On every side there still remains the handiwork of these men of the old time, their garden plots, their burial mounds, their cattle enclosures and their hillside forts and settlements. When I come out of my house to walk on any of these high grassy tracks it is not the ploughed lands or the feeble fences that dominate the earth's surface here. In every direction the skyline is broken by barrows that all day long under the light of the sun and all night long under the light of the moon raise their round breasts to the outer spaces.

In a nearby valley under Bats Head can be seen the very plan of a Neolithic village, the round floors of the huts still, after so many thousands of years, uninvaded by the surrounding grass and with each boundary bank of the hillside allotment fields clearly defined. Here, to the left is the constructed pathway down which these dwellers returned after their inland hunting expeditions, here in the valley bottom the deep shaft they dug still unfilled. Far above on the hill's crest obtrude the enormous banks of their cattle enclosure, grown over now with nettles and thorn trees and yet solid and actual for all to see. High against the skyline to the east rises Flower's Barrow, an entrenched hilltop camp overlooking Worbarrow Bay, and with the ruined outline of Lulworth Castle set amongst its trees, as it were in some old engraving. Flower's Barrow represents a strategic settlement of these early peoples guarding the Island of Purbeck. The downland track leading to Maiden Castle, the largest earthwork in the world, passed near to it. But it must not be concluded that these strongholds, improved and fortified by the warrior Celts, were originally built for military purpose.

It is clear that for thousands of years men and women lived out their lives with no conception of organised warfare. These trading folk of Megalithic times, who first spread abroad the traditions of agricultural stability amongst the rude hunters and food-gatherers of the island, built up and preserved for countless centuries an archaic civilisation of peaceful intentions such as has never been repeated. Small wonder that we call out to each other still to touch wood at moments of our lives when we suspect Fate of treachery. The ages of wood and stone were friendly ages.

How thrilling to the imagination it is to see lying exposed before your eyes on the muddy furrows some perfect specimen of the earliest craft of man's hand! There it lies—a scraper, a saw, a knife, an arrow head formed out of this indestructible substance, exactly as it was, down to the tiniest secondary working when it was first made. It comes to you as a token, a living message directly across the thousands of intervening years. It *was* and it *is* again. For this time-space it has been hidden away in a mindless oblivion awaiting the hour when its existence will once more be consciously recognised. It is taken into the hand and immediately the ingenuity of its artificial conformation, the result of long hours of workmanship, bridges with a shock of reality the interval between then and now. To look for worked flints is like looking for jewels.

It is of course an unwise undertaking to try to formulate with too much precision the working methods of this oldest craft. Since early man first took a stone into his hand with the definite purpose of shaping it to his use the selected processes by which he achieved his end have been various. In these days it is difficult to appreciate the enormous advance that the mastery of wood and stone marks in the history of human development. Man's deft fingers are fitted with thin plates of horn, and yet how feeble in contrast to the claws of a bear or tiger. His mouth is provided with teeth, and yet how harmless. How handicapped he, of necessity, would be if compelled to rely upon this natural equipment alone. He requires a stick for a bow an arrow; he must break it either by force or by a twisting method and make uniform its splintered end as best he can with his teeth—yet with a flint saw the matter is effected in a moment with perfect precision. His fist is of value to him, and yet how far more formidable would his hand be when grasping a well-balanced hand-axe. Again, when his quarry lay at his feet, how impossible to take off the skin or hide of it effectively by biting and tearing. With a sharp flint instrument the thing could be done with the most express competence.

Such an astounding advance over the animal world is implicit in the free use of wood and stone that it is small wonder men were content with the exploitation of their discovery for hundreds of thousands of years. There is no doubt that they made use of flint and bone and wood every hour of their lives. They crushed, they cut, they scraped, they punched, they sowed instruments of their own manipulation. Their flaking was done for the most part with a hammer stone. The most perfect one of them that I have I came upon on the sheep-cropped turf of the downs only a few feet from my house. Of the implements generally known as 'Thomas picks' I have found no less than six, all of them shaped identically. These were possibly hafted and used as adzes for hollowing out timber. A tool that must have been very much in use was a scraper, of which I have found hundreds. They were required for cleaning the insides of skins as a preliminary for stretching them out in the sun. They vary considerably in form and size.

I have also found a great number of rough arrowheads but only a single perfect one with its tangs unbroken. There are large quantities of rough arrowheads too ill-made and unshapely to be of any practical use for archery; the true purpose of these was, I believe, as teeth set into boards of some kind of rough carding or thrashing process. Spearheads are comparatively rare. The most perfect specimen I have, as happens with many flints, has been re-chopped a second time after its original manufacture, perhaps being found and retouched after an interval of several thousand years. I also have knives with handles for possible hafting, some of them of exactly the same shape, like a dinner service. A large saw I possess was probably set in wood and used for cutting branches for clubs and bows, and a spoke shave for rubbing the bark off a stick by friction. The puncher or borer, of which I have a great quantity, was used for making holes in skins or piercing bone. Among my most interesting finds were the pigmy flints which have always puzzled antiquarians. They were perhaps used for ceremonial purposes or as toys to amuse children.

The wheat-growing surface soil of these ploughlands does not go down very deep. A foot or two and one comes to the hard chalk. It is for this reason that no instrument, implement or weapon of flint dropped by man, from the earliest time when these eternal hills first rose out of the sea, can ever be lost. In the classical ages these 'thunder-stones' were thought to have fallen from heaven, while in the Middle Ages they were called 'elf-shot', and were considered as the authentic ammunition of pert elves when they were warring. It is for this reason that they have always been regarded as lucky, and are still often treasured by boys and girls who are innocent of all knowledge of their origin.

In truth there is something mysterious about them. How could it be otherwise! Consider the innumerable winter nights when a crystal coldness was upon these fields, hour after hour, and they lying undisturbed. Consider the summer dog days and they still waiting. When the angels called to the shepherds on the hills at Bethlehem these modest fragments were in the same secret mould. They were here in Dorset when Alexander the Great captured Tyre, when the Assyrians returned from their forages like the Doones of the desert, their chariots weighted down with the blood-stained human skins of their enemies. The tiniest chip, the most insignificant scratch remains on a flint forever. Presently, as the varied forms grow familiar, one learns to appreciate and understand the purpose of each of them. In this way these simple stones preserve in a most exact fashion the expression of intelligent thought, and though the minds that have moulded them have suffered so long an annihilation, the intention that prompted those vanished fingers of dust lasts on.

Guests of Grace

If I lie quiet in my bedroom I often hear a low murmuring sound as of distant voices in the streets of a populous city. It is the murmur of bees. Two years ago they came clustering over the downs, and discovering a hole in one of the flints of which our cottage is built, entered their spacious chambers under our bedroom floor. The hole was no larger than an old woman's thimble, yet since that day in June this insignificant crevice has become a golden thoroughfare to a golden citadel. This eye of a needle serves the turn of the bees most satisfactorily. It can be easily defended against marauders and it gives entrance to long symmetrical sequestered galleries far surpassing in design and extent any hollows that could be provided by the aged oak trees in Lulworth Park, 'with high top, bald with dry antiquity'.

The publican and the carpenter of the village, both of them keen and competent bee masters, would have me take up the boards of my room, capture the swarm, and house it in more conventional quarters. This suggestion has never appealed to me. To whose pent-house shall these sacred insects come if not to the eaves of such a faithful worshipper of the sun as I have declared myself to be all my life long?

The word 'bee' has a very ancient origin. It derives through the Anglo-Saxon from the Aryan word 'bhi' which meant to quiver, for our early ancestors had always noted how exquisitely the silver wings of these noon-day couriers shivered in the bright sunshine. What a parterre of peace and industry is presented to our minds by the word 'bee-garden', and how lovely to lie dreaming in such an enclosure with the hum of these dedicated creatures everywhere about us! Surely they are God's very children and it is no sun-bonnet hearsay that they will show choler at the approach of the mean, whereas a free and generous spirit will seldom become a victim to their saucy scimitars.

The ancients used to deliver many strange statements about bees. The best way to stimulate multiplication, they thought, was by burying the carcase of an ox in the earth with nothing but his horns showing above the ground. It was then only necessary, on a hot summer's day, to saw off the ends of these horns, when up through two narrow passages thus opened a full swarm would emerge in an unending procession. When an old woman runs out beating her frying pans together—who of her neighbours realises that they are listening to the very cymbals struck in the immemorial worship of Demeter!

Strange truly are the secrets contained in a common skep of straw at the back of a kitchen garden where the horse-radish grows. Who shall explain the nature of the implacable far-seeing spirit of the hive? By what impossible social mandate is the hive so infallibly organized? These scrupulous dainty ravishers of the lime-tree blossoms, of the charlock, of the white clover, of the horseshoe vetch, of the heather, should be able to rouse us out of our spiritual apathy any hour of a summer's morning. It has always been counted a fortunate thing to have one's roof-tree selected by a flight of wild bees as a permanent domicile and I think he would be a man of little prudence or poetry, indeed, no well-descended spirit, who would grudge free entertainment to such eager and obedient children of the unvanquished sun.

Robert Herrick

All critics agree that Robert Herrick has written some of the most graceful lyrics to be found in the English language, but the same consensus of opinion does not extend to the poet's character or outlook on life. Conventional people have always been inclined to put aside his 'unbaptized rhymes' as mere literary exercises written to please Saint Ben of 'the mountain belly and rocky face', and having little to do with the 'real' Herrick—the devout cavalier parson, whose political persuasions were so sound, and whose verses in *Noble Numbers* testify to his having been so wholesome an expositor of Church of England doctrines.

> To his Book's end this last line he'd have plac't,
> Jocund his Muse was; but his life was chast.

Some support may perhaps be found for this apologia from the fact that Herrick's playful prayers and half-serious litanies were remembered in the cottages of Devonshire for more than a hundred years after his death. In the year 1809 a curious visitor questioned the village people of Dean Prior about their former parson and was astonished to discover that there was living an old woman of over ninety who could recite without a trip the religious hymn 'To His Angrie God', which opens with the truly terrifying lines

> Through all the night
> Thou dost me fright.

This story surely would seem to suggest that Herrick's parish duties had not been neglected and that his congregation had been duly impressed by his devotional versifications, seeing that it was their own earthen pot heads which for a period preserved the literary immortality of their clergyman.

Hesperides was published a little before King Charles was beheaded and was then forgotten until rediscovered by a certain Mr Nichols at the end of the eighteenth century. The frontispiece of the original edition is embellished with the head of the author engraved by William Marshall. It is very well known, and in all probability represents a passing good likeness, for Marshall had already done a similar service for Bacon, Donne and Milton. Of a Roman cast, heavy and gross, it is difficult to believe that the profile on the faded page could possibly represent the countenance of the poet. The picture, however, helps us to understand how the coarser verses in *Hesperides* came to be written, those satirical quatrains and clever couplets composed after the manner of Martial, smelling more of sack than the lamp and which are apt to disgust even those writers who affect a preference for broad and honest speech.

> Wither'd with yeeres, and bed-rid Mumma lyes;
> Dry-rosted all, but raw yet in her eyes.

Or again:

> Ralph pares his nayles, his warts, his cornes, and Ralph
> In several tills, and boxes keepes 'em safe;
> Instead of Harts-horne (if he speakes the troth)
> To make a lustie-gellie for his broth.

The fact is that Herrick was not the pious George Herbert-like country cavalier parson that the orthodox wish to believe him to have been, nor on the other hand was he intent on directing the minds of his readers to the contemplation of human scurf and nothing else. He was religious as are those who venerate the tradition and usages of antiquity, but at the same time upon occasions he could display a pagan heartlessness to suffering and a pagan contempt for all that is uncomely or old.

The vigour of his 'brutish sting', symbolised by his prodigious nose in the picture, was powerful enough (and this a strange anomaly) to refine rather than roughen his spirit, rendering his fancy light and volatile as a sycamore seed, and curing him of that blinkered use and wanton stare with which almost all men regard women. This Robin Hood the second owed homage to two worlds—the actual world of his day-by-day activities where he lived as a favoured bachelor priest with Prudence Baldwin to cook for but not 'to cocker his appetite' in the old vicarage of Dean Prior; and the world of his imagination, the enchanted Forest of Arden, a kind of land of Shee that any Jacobean Miss could in an instant conjure up for him. These two worlds, both of them deeply poetical, acted as foils the one to the other.

Although in Herrick's time a certain amount of weaving was done at Dean Prior, the village for the most part supported itself as it does today from the produce of its orchards and pasture lands. It is situated five miles from Totnes in the fertile valley of the Dart with the tors of the moor clearly visible from its churchyard. In the seventeenth century the only approach to the vicarage was along a winding, leafy lane. At the end of this Midsummer-Eve lane, deep embowered amid forests of apple trees, were the Church glebe lands of ninety and more acres irrigated by 'leats' from the stream called Dean Burn. It was in these fat acres that Herrick's 'great-ey'd kine' were to be seen grazing, and in the uplands nearer the moor, his sheep.

> Here thou behold'st thy large sleek Neat
> Unto the Dew-laps up in meat...
>
> These seen, thou go'st to view thy flocks
> Of sheep, (safe from the Wolfe and Fox)
> And find'st their bellies there as full
> Of short sweet grasse, as backs with wool.

In one of his most winning poems entitled 'A Thanksgiving to God for his house' he has with pretty artifice presented an unforgettable picture of the Arcadian husbandry of his dwelling.

> Low is my porch, as is my Fate,
>> Both void of state;
> And ye the threshold of my doore
>> Is worn by th' poore.
>
> Lord, I confess, too, when I dine,
>> The Pulse is Thine,
> And all those other Bits, that bee
>> There placed by Thee,
> The Worts, the Purslain, and the Messe
>> Of water-cresse.
>
> Like as my Parlour so my Hall
>> And Kitchin's small:
> A little Butterie, and therein
>> A little Byn ...

This then was the solid, sensible background of his life in Devonshire. So solid, indeed, was the structure of the old vicarage that much of it still stands today, and that it might be conceivably possible for a painstaking mason, on any Saturday afternoon of the present year, to exhume from its crannied sepulchre in the kitchen wall the skeleton, parched and brittle, of one of the many crickets which had used to act 'the music of the feast' to Herrick as, with his old friend Jacky Wickes by a bright fire in the chimney nook, he read of the Trojan War.

> When the faire Hellen, from her eyes,
> Shot forth her loving Sorceries:
>> At which Ile reare
> Mine aged limbs above my chaire:
>> And hearing it,
> Flutter and crow, as in a fit
> Of fresh concupiscence, and cry,
> 'No lust there's like to poetry'.

Season followed season as the broken times approached rolling the poet in chariots of blossom towards the oblivion he dreaded. Each year when the Hock-cart brought the last sheaf home to Sir Edward Giles's barton grange Herrick would be following behind with the revellers, and he would be present also to christen the trees with 'lamb's-wool' from the wassail bowl, leaving the warmth of the parlour to perform this ancient twelfth night obligation under the orchard stars, devising on his return 'mirth to dulcet man's miseries', as eager as the elected King and Queen to play at Fox-in-the-hole. For as he himself admits he was a confirmed bachelor:

> Ile hug, Ile kisse, Ile play
> And Cock-like, Hens Ile tread;
> And sport it any way,
> But in the Bridall Bed.

But most blithe of all would he be at that time of year when little children begin to drop violets on the halter-paths and the daffodils, one behind the other, open their yellow separate trumpets under sheltered walls. Then as the days lengthened, with rooks cawing in the elm tree tops, and blackbirds each night at a later hour whistling in the hedges, the mere glimpse of Mistress Julia, of Mistress Elizabeth Wheeler, of Mistress Amy Potter, of Mistress Lettice Yarde, would scatter all his thoughts, instantly admitting him to his 'pipkin paradise', a paradise real and unreal, where sights and sounds and smells suffered a strange heightening, and where tansy cakes tasted like the bread of Adonis, and the sense of touch was beyond words swooning sweet. It was then that this black-headed curly-locks was tamed of his bestialities, was rendered 'ayrie, active to be born, like Iphyclus, upon the tops of corn', able to change the lust of the goat into a grace as light and delicate as that of butterflies trembling in ecstasy at the end of a dry, grassy pennant. Was it perhaps on some lazy Sunday afternoon towards the end of August that Julia was subjected to the depredations of two filching snatch-thieves as she lay amongst the fallen fruit, warm and wasp-eaten, in the long grass of the lower vicarage orchard?

> As Julia once a-slumb'ring lay,
> It chanc't a Bee did flie that way,
> (After a dew, or dew-like shower)
> To tipple freely in a flower.
> For some rich flower, he took the lip
> Of Julia, and began to sip ...

> I thought I might there take a taste,
> When so much sirrop ran at waste.

From chin to ankle there was no part of a young girl's body that did not make Herrick mad with mortal longings. Each cool shadow, lying so softly on the flesh of these fair creatures, was an irresistible enticement to him to dangle his soul upon the sea-saw of desire. Every inch of a girl's body was to him worshipful and charged with a peculiar lustre. He looks passionately upon it in its plain carnality, striving to recreate it in an airy sort, out of spring flowers, as Welsh mythology teaches us happened to the maiden Blodeuwedd. These lively, lovely girls, shy and liquid-eyed as new-born calves in his own strawy cowshed, wayward as the dapple deer half hidden in the ferns of Sir Edward Giles's park, full of duplicity as nesting ploughland lapwings, could in a trice translate him body and soul into a horse-shoe fairy world substantial enough for treading, and for ravishing sensations, and yet ethereal too, as though belonging to some old fabled country of Master Malory' s invention where nothing had been mapped out but 'damaskt meadowes', shining rivers, and pavilions of chivalry!

These ladies of dainty dalliance fluttered all day long before his eyes like wanton fuchsia flowers, beyond all measure provocative, with their uptilted petal frocks; so that when he lay down at night he remained under the same glamour bewildered with the fantasy prospect of an exacting venery. There never lived a poet who has more sanely and yet more gaily expressed the pretty rewards and pastimes of true love.

> If I kisse Anthea's brest
> There I smell the Phenix nest ...

And yet how delicate is his poem addressed to the nipples on Julia's breast:

> Have ye beheld (with much delight),
> A red-Rose peeping through a white?
> Or else a Cherrie (double grac't),
> Within a Lillie-center plac't?

Herrick's sensuality is of a complexion so unabashed and generous that without effort he attains to that high state of heroical love passion when nothing that belongs to the body of the loved one can be anything but precious. This is a madness reserved for the true nurslings of Dionysus, fox children, whose blood moves like the tides every day of the week towards one central garden of Allah.

> Wo'd ye oyle of Blossomes get?
> Take it from my Julia's sweat;
> Oyl of Lillies, and of Spike,
> From her moysture take the like.

Not one of Herrick's five senses but is used to deepen the emotions he experiences as he penetrates further and further along the rain-soft mossy paths, smelling of the sappy juice of bluebells and 'tinseled with twilight', of his secret garden.

> Shew me thy feet; shew me thy legs, thy thighes;
> Shew me Those Fleshie Principalities;
> Shew me the Hill (where smiling Love doth sit) ...

To a discerning reader the beautiful but studied verses in *Noble Numbers* form no serious stumbling block to the belief that Herrick alone of all the English poets is a true amoral hedonist after the ancient classical manner. He does not hesitate to give Christianity itself a pagan turn, and when he writes of the Nativity it is as though he regretted that Jesus had not been a favoured sylvan brat suckled gypsy-fashion under a dog-rose Devonshire hedge.

> Instead of neat Inclosures
> Of inter-woven Osiers;
> Instead of fragrant Posies
> Of Daffodils, and Roses:
> Thy cradle, Kingly Stranger,
> As Gospell tells,
> Was nothing els,
> But, here, a homely manger.

Sir Edmund Gosse believed that in the days of his early manhood Herrick had a bastard child by Julia. To Mistress Thomasin Parsons, the pretty daughter of Mr John Parsons, organist and master of the choristers at Westminster Abbey, we know he wrote these lines:

If thou aske me (Dear) wherefore
I do write of thee no more:
I must answer (sweet) thy part
Less is here then in my heart.

It is likely enough that the musician's two daughters were amongst the fair visitors who used to come to the West Country in the summer months, and it may well have been in a cowslip field that these lovely lines to Thomasin were written:

Grow up in beauty, as thou do'st begin,
And be of all admired, Tomasin.

Archbishop Laud in his attempt to bring the clergy under a stricter discipline inaugurated a system of espionage. There is extant a state paper belonging to the year 1640 in which these significant words are to be read:

Thomsen Parsons hath had a Bastard lately; shee was brought to bed at Greenwch, Mr Herrisque a minister possest of a very good Living in Devonshire hath not resided there haveing noe lycence for his non residence and not being Chapline to any Noble man or man qualified by law as I heare, his lodging is at Westminster, in the little Amrie at Nikolas Wilkes his house where the said Thomsen Parsons lives.

As those whose religion it is to worship life are apt to do, Robert Herrick lived to a great age. The last written record of him is to be found in the parish register of Dean Prior. Here are the rueful words:

ROBERT HERRICK, VICKER, WAS
BURIED YE 15TH DAY OF OCTOBER, 1674

There his bones lie in that old Devonshire churchyard wrapped fast in their shroud, the bones of a Clerk in Holy Orders who could have better led a Bacchanalian rout than serve at a Christian altar.

The Body is the soules poore house, or home
Whose Ribs the laths are, and whose Fleshe the loame.

Thus they have lain under the shadow of that fine embattlemented tower while the petals of two-hundred-and-sixty one generations of celandines have turned from gold to silver in the ditches, and as many generations of winter field rats have sought the shelter of barley mows. His sermons are forgot, no text of them remains, and yet like hints out of a far past punctiliously preserved in the matrices of agates his wisdom has come down to us.

South Somerset Names

In the wall near the porch of Chilthorne Domer church, Somerset, there may be seen traces of a primitive sundial. I noticed these marks first when I was with my father. Standing side by side in the small country graveyard, so uneven from its green grass mounds and so sequestered, we contemplated together these scratches on the grey masonry, scratches that once had scrupulously registered the fugitive hours of far-off medieval Holy Days. Suddenly my father spoke: 'I hope, Llewelyn my boy, that you will live to do good in your generation'. The unexpected words must have made some impression on me or my mind would never have preserved as clearly as it does the memory of that particular autumn afternoon—the sound of chattering starlings on the church roof, the smell of hidden-away apple orchards, and, over all, the blackberry-blue mists of Somerset. Yet how could the words 'in your generation' be understood by me in the careless heyday of my youth? Nobody under the age of thirty years ever truly comprehends the brevity of human life.

It is not till we have lived for over half a century that the ephemeral nature of our existence really becomes lodged in our feckless heads. When Apollo and Poseidon were being cheated of their proper wage by the father of Priam after they had sweated the very fat off their bones at building of the great walls of Troy, the Sun-God remarked petulantly to the great Sea-God: 'Why should we stand here haggling any longer, or indeed have anything whatever to do with this contemptible race which lasts no longer than leaves!'

In the bustle of our own work-a-day lives, with day following day, month following month, the foolish illusion of permanence becomes more and more obstinately convincing, and it is only under the discipline of some cursed sickness, or when startled out of our spiritual sloth by sudden death, that we begin really and truly to apprehend the unpleasing truth that was contained in the wrothful words of the cozened deity. Century follows century and the generations rise and fall until it sometimes seems that only by tradition is a semblance of duration preserved. Especially is this the case with the names that linger in an historic locality. Races may come and races may go, but the same airy syllables will be still upon the lips of men and women from millenium to millenium. Such long-surviving place-names give a reassuring continuity to the mortal processions that go trooping towards dusty death, working, laughing and love-making, in their successive predestined periods. Often if we examine them the names that we use reveal a surprisingly accurate observation of a landscape the contours of which have become so much a familiar background of our own lives that it is difficult to conceive of them as having been so narrowly known and scrutinised by the men of the old time.

Consider some of the names of the villages around Yeovil. Chiselborough is derived from the Old English words *Ceosol-beorg* (gravel hill), a reference doubtless to that diminutive mountain, topped with Scotch firs, that is so conspicuous a landmark from Ham Hill above Jack O'Beards, or to travellers crossing the Parrett on the road from Norton to Crewkerne. It is interesting to notice here that the same word *Ceosol* was used by the Anglo-Saxons to denote the Chesil

Beach—the celebrated sea-bank that for countless ages has protected Dorset from the violence of the huge ocean waves sweeping into the West Bay from the Atlantic. To those of us who have recollections of bathing in the Yeo near Mudford how admirably chosen seems the ancient name of that water-meadow village, as well selected as Witcombe was for the hamlet that lies on the edge of the droves and dykes and bottoms below the village of Ash—a name that originally meant the valley of the willows. In the fields beneath the beautiful village of Trent, with its meandering streets and its church spire so gracefully visible amongst shady trees, there are to be found autumn crocuses or naked nannies, a most delicate flower, which, perhaps, owes its presence to the water-soaked nature of those pastures. The name of the village, Trent, is derived from the name of the stream that flows through it, a name which in the British tongue meant 'trespasser', and was descriptive of water that was liable to flood.

The Chinnocks get their name from the old English word *cinu*, meaning a fissure or ravine, and this also seems appropriate to those of us who have been used to approach them from the north, down lovely deep-sunken lanes that rattle with hazel nuts in the autumn and in April smell so sweet of primroses, with linnets nesting everywhere in golden gorse above the steep sandstone banks.

The etymology of Crewkerne may be found in the British word *cruc* (hill), referring to the characteristic topography of the place, Crewkerne literary meaning 'The house at Cruc'. Odcombe receives from the *Oxford Dictionary of Place Names* two possible derivations—'Uda's comb or valley' or from the Old English *wudu-cumb*—'wood coomb'—an explanation I prefer since it brings back to my mind more vividly the steep-shadowed road that winds up to the 'hungry air' of the windy village after you have left the Galpin's Lodge and Primrose Cottage behind you, a way travelled so often by Nancy Cooper and her daughter in rain and sleet and sun and shower.

In Switzerland in the depth of the summer it is the custom to graze the cattle on the tops of the mountains, milking and herding them there for as long as there is no snow. Somerton, we are informed, is derived from the Old English *Sumor-tun*—summer dwelling—and denoted a place to which cattle were taken and to which people went during the warmer months of the year. A suggestion of the same kind of pastoral procedure is contained in the name Henstridge, near

Stalbridge, which comes from the Old English word *hengest*, 'stallion'—i.e. 'the ridge where stallions were kept'.

In the hunting diaries that my uncle Littleton wrote describing his adventures with the Blackmore Vale eighty years ago, Henstridge Ash is often mentioned, for even timber is privileged to enjoy a more reasonable longevity than is man, man whose life lasts scarcely longer than the grass of the fields. The walnut tree in the glebe of Montacute Vicarage, whose well-proportioned comely form and cool enfolded bough-branched arbours have revived the spirits and given quiet to the minds of I know not how many pedestrians walking up the Station Hill, stands today as familiar and unchanged as in my childhood; and although five decades have passed since my nursery walks, and the Squire and Deborah Sparkes, and my mother and father, and Colin Harding, and Job Dunston, and Charles Childs now lie buried in the churchyard, I can detect no alteration in the splendour of the great sycamore tree which each morning and evening casts so noble a shadow across the Abbey Pond.

> Says the old man to oak tree:
> Young and lusty was I when first I knew thee;
> I was young and lusty, I was strong and fair;
> Young and lusty was I many a long year;
> But sadly failed am I, sadly fail'd now,
> Sadly fail'd am I since I first knew thou.

Hedgecock Memories

Although in the familiar outline of the Montacute hills, Hedgecock, sheltered as it is between Miles Hill and Ham Hill, takes a somewhat inconspicuous place in the landscape, it is an eminence by no means to be despised. This shaggy mountain, though no less prominent than its two neighbours, is, as its name implies, wilder than they and for all that it does not flaunt its presence, its bosky conical shape is sufficiently familiar to West Country people; to bagmen coming down over Babylon Hill into Yeovil; to shepherds crow-barring hurdle-holes on Corton Downs; to back-door hen-wives on the Polden Hills; to eel-spearers on Sedgemoor anxious for the end of their water-net work; and to clod-weary ploughmen turning a final furrow on the airy uplands of High Ham. Miles Hill, it cannot be denied, has played a far more notable part in English history than ever Hedgecock has done. Around its manifest earth-trenched summit there has been gathered, through the centuries, a wealth of legendary lore only rivalled perhaps in the West by that of Glastonbury Tor and Cadbury Camp.

The distinction of Hedgecock is not such an obvious one, its romantic appeal resting less upon popular fame than upon the secret grace of its own sequestered dells and leafy unvisited hollows. Even as late as a quarter of a century ago Hedgecock Forest flourished in all its original woodland glory. To the right of the mud track that leads to Ham Hill, at the top of the first dip, there used to grow one of the finest beech trees I have ever seen in my life. Towering up and up, branch above branch, in all the splendour of its maturity, it had played for generations the part of a faithful trysting tree for all true lovers. 'Come, woo me, woo me; for now I am in a holiday humour and like enough to consent'. The timber of the Forest of Arden was all scratched about, so it is rumoured, with love messages, and the silvered coating of smooth white bark of this giant beech presented a kind of palimpsest *Domesday Book* of the names of all the sweethearts who had trodden over the dog's-mercury and primroses of the wood since Queen Victoria first came to the throne. Often I have wondered into whose possession that huge trunk came after the woodcutters had felled it. In what lumber-merchant's yard did it lie unhonoured, except perhaps by humble rural working-men whose imaginations had never been dulled by the deceits of gain? Skeat instructs us that the original books were 'pieces of writing scratched on a beechen board', the Anglo-Saxon word *boc* meaning book and also beech tree. What a book that huge bole could have been for a wise man's reading, a text that offered an infallible testimony to the mystery of life, with love-knots and arrow-pierced hearts uniting the parents and grandparents of half that Arcadian locality!

When I was a little boy it was a common sight to see red squirrels in the trees of Hedgecock, but in later years these active chattering arboreal little animals disappeared altogether, perhaps hunted down with the stones and catapults of Bishopston urchins, or destroyed, for all I know, by one of those sinister pestilences that periodically infect the rodent world. The following rhyme suggests the plentiful amount of timber that used to grow along this easterly salient of the greater Ham Hill promontory in the old days: 'From Ham Stone to Dog-trap Lea, a squirrel can leap from tree to tree.' The Ham Stone referred to was a colossal projection of oolithic sandstone that stood, I believe, a little southward of The Prince of Wales Inn. This remarkable natural monument—the 'girt Ham Stone', as it was called in the district—had survived since the original geological formation of the ancient leonine hill. It must have been known to the early Britons, have been as familiar to the Roman soldiery as to the medieval quarrymen. Indeed, it was not demolished till almost within memory of man; sold, so Dr Hensleigh Walter informed me, to a common road-contractor to be broken up.

But if the trees of the hill have sheltered together with squirrels, hawks, rooks and sentinel jays, the ground beneath their roots has provided excellent dens for badgers and foxes. With enormous platforms before each earth, platforms heightened and broadened by the renewed excavations of successive breeding seasons, these cunning four-footed creatures dwell in relative security at the very top of Hedgecock, having need to give attention to few sounds other than the rustlings of rabbits, the crowing of cock-pheasants, and wind in the trees.

As boys my brother Willie and I would sometimes be invited to go rabbiting in Hedgecock with Captain Chaffey. Followed by Crook the coachman, with a bottle of Burgundy, chicken sandwiches and bread and cheese, we would start away full of eagerness from East Stoke House, destined often, as it fell out, to do little else than to keep watch and ward for what seemed interminable hours outside rabbit holes in the hope of recovering a truant ferret that was regaling itself at its leisure, or perhaps even sleeping, at the further end of some inaccessible subterranean gallery. Bob Chaffey was a character not easy to be matched, a lovable sort of Uncle Toby, with an innocent dry humour of his own private invention as natural as it was droll. He was indeed a typical product of the English countryside, an old-fashioned gentleman—stubborn, sympathetic and proud, modest, egocentric and kindly.

Only on one occasion do I recall his straying from the *Tao* natural to his amenable temperament, and this happened under my own ill influence. We had been out one afternoon and *shot nothing*. It was a mild day towards the end of January and we were resting on a fallen tree trunk in the very heart of Hedgecock, idly listening to a cock blackbird that, at the first hint of softer weather, had begun to sing in the rays of leaf-level sunlight, with the full-throated ecstasy of the springtime.

Hither my love!
Here I am! here!

This gentle call is for you, my love, you.
Do not be decoyed elsewhere,
That is the whistle of the wind, it is not my voice,
That is the fluttering, the fluttering of the spray,
Those are the shadows of leaves.

The whole wintry wood was held under a glamour by the bird's passion, not a branch stirred, not a twig trembled. And then Satan whispered slyly into my schoolboy ear to persuade Captain Chaffey to shoot this winged creature that thought itself safe so high above our heads. At first he would have nothing to do with so dastardly a plan, but I pleaded and pleaded with him until the moment arrived when the harmless happy hedge-fowl lay at my feet with red blood upon its golden bill. I do not believe the ancient mariner was as conscience-stricken over the killing of the albatross as was my companion over the death of this common cock blackbird. 'I ought never to have done it,' he kept repeating, and the remorse that he showed all the way home imprinted the incident upon my memory, together with a sense of shame that I feel to this day.

No one was more sensitive to, or indeed quicker to appreciate the peculiar qualities of the people he had to do with than was Captain Chaffey. There are those who would like all the world to be of one fashion. The inhabitants of Stoke and Montacute never subscribed to this; rich and poor alike, they have always been renowned for their singularities, for being, shall we say, a trifle 'out of the ordinary'; and the eccentric landowner relished these eccentric ones as much as they did him. The Yeovil-Ilminster road used to be at the beginning of the century enlivened by the presence of a little jobber named Hawkins. This man almost every day could be seen driving from his cottage somewhere beyond John Walter's house, with its Fives Courts and stag in the garden, into Montacute. His conveyance consisted of a home-made cart scarcely bigger than a goat-carriage, which, pasted all over with Bible texts, drawn forward by a donkey and usually filled to the brim with laughing children, whom the jolly little good poor man had taken along with him for company's sake.

Another character who was an especial favourite with my friend lived in a cottage near the gates of his drive. This was an octogenarian labourer called Denman who understood life, and the poetry of life, better than many who were far more learned. He had indeed a pure and most original genius that broke through the crust of the commonplace every hour of the day. All those shallow importunate surface impressions that render most of us as stupid as stockfish he looked upon with an illuminated God-given imagination. His everyday talk was thick with poetry, with poetry that sounded as natural as wind and water. He was a man with hands that were horn-hard from a life of toil. His hair and beard were snow-white, and standing under the copper beech, a tree always so eloquent of well-to-do garden securities, he would speak to me like one of the ancient prophets, like the prophet Amos under his wild sycamore. 'His word was in mine heart as a burning fire shut up in my bones, and I was weary with forbearing and I could not stay'. After I had left him I would sometimes write down what he had said. One of those far-off mornings reads as follows: 'Sixty years agone today come two months, I were a'traipsing along this here turnpike to ploughing match. Yes, we know as much of life as they that cross the ocean, *we that live on the deep soil*. We have our waves, as we was the rest of 'em, we quarrymen and ploughmen, come fine, come sleet, come cold, come het.'

Montacute Mills

One of the pleasantest of the walks in the neighbourhood of the village of Montacute in Somerset is the one which leads across the park to the old mill. This solid structure, which so often catches the sunshine upon door and hatch, no longer serves the purpose for which it was built. It stands in silence by a grass-grown lane deserted now by everything but rabbits, foxes or an occasional turnip-put.

What the quern used to be to the household, the manorial mill was to the economy of the village. No mill, no meal. The importance of these centres of agrarian husbandry may easily be estimated when we recall that those in existence at the time of the Norman Conquest were all recorded in the *Domesday Book*. Indeed at school we used to be taught that King William's Great Inquisition of the land of England was so thorough as even to concern itself with so inconsiderable a mill as that one-horse house that still continues to grind Dorset corn half a mile below Sherborne bridge.

The process of converting grain to flour has at all times and in all places given easy occasion for dishonesty. There exist sayings in almost every language testifying to a universal suspicion of these masters of the most necessary of all trades. Whenever, in Dorset, children catch sight of a puss-moth, a moth whose head, body and fore-wings have about them a white fluffy look suggestive, so it has been thought, of a powdery miller busy among his gunny bags, they will sing in mocking tones:

> Millery, millery, dousty pole!
> How many zacks hast thee a-stole?
> Vour and twenty in a peck
> Hang the miller up by's neck!

Many proverbs have come down to us that give rough expression to this popular distrust. 'As stout as a miller's collar that takes a thief by the neck each morning', or again, 'Put a miller, a weaver, and a tailor in a bag, shake them well, and the first that comes out will be a thief'.

Behind Montacute Mill, no longer humming to jolly revolutions of a huge hopper-stone, there stands a most charmed spinney. In my childhood rooks rested in this copse, and the endless clamour of the birds in springtime seemed to add to the life of the lovely little wood, floored white and gold with garlic and marybuds, flowers which were destined to be, as the summer strengthened, entirely overlaid by enormous burdock leaves whose broadness, outstretching the ears of African elephants, screened every inch of the soggy ground with umbrellas green and sun-proof, three or even four feet high.

In mid-winter how remarkably all this was changed! It was then that the hollow, deep-banked stream of Lufton and Thorn Coffin, swollen by innumerable tributaries, tinkling, trickling from field and furrow, would brim the stone-walled mill pond to overflowing, causing a weighty waterfall to come swirling through the sluice, days before being raised to its highest notch by the weather-wise miller's man.

At such flood times it was a happiness for us to stand below on a splashed grassy promontory watching the falling thunder of this cascade, which, arched like the broad neck of a shire stallion, hurled itself into the gloomy water-wheel pool with a violence and deafening riot that were destined to impress my imagination far more deeply than anything I was later to see at Niagara, where, holding fast to a branch of an alder tree on Goat Island, I once contemplated the rapids of the celebrated cataract.

I had learned by heart on one of those schoolroom mornings of my childhood William Allingham's poem of the fairies which began:

Up the airy mountain,
Down the rushy glen,
We daren't go a-hunting
For fear of little men.

These verses were never to be dissociated from the 'Columbkill lights' on the perishable foam bubbles that chance had delivered from the wild turbulence of the mid-stream current, to pause uneasily for a hazardous moment under the bank at our very feet, shivering, shimmering with all the colours of peacock and rainbow upon their airy evanescent globes.

How lovely these small meadow-streams of Somerset can be in the summer, streams that are the watery dwelling places of gluttonous eels whose naked creature flesh, clapped close to drowned sticks, to caddisworm mud, nurses in its mysterious serpent's heart fateful yearnings for a deep-sea darkness that has nothing to do with the come-day-go-day of their frog-feeding, freshwater lives; streams that shelter loaches, fish learned in the matter of under-stone lurking places—slippery, secretive and barbelled at the chin; streams whose rushy shallows are everywhere crinkled with schools of sticklebacks, little silver slips with flickering flanks, bright shining as christening spoons; streams that flow indolently on and on, under willow, and hazel, and alder, towards the idle, dragonfly-haunted, waterlily-warm reaches of the River Parrett.

In the gusty fields that lie below Windmill Farm, plovers wail and wheel all day long, and there where the stream is scarcely too wide for the frolic prance of a lamb, cowslips can be gathered by the cap and apron full.

Tissty tossty one and twenty,
How many years shall I live hearty?

If anyone starting from those fields of tall cowslips has the resolution to follow down the course of the small stream, past the burdock spinney, through the meadows below the Montacute railway station and across Marsh Lane, he will presently come upon, in a countryside of indescribable seclusion, a second mill—Wulham's Mill! It resembles a small but very ancient farmhouse with sagging moss-grown roof, a farmhouse that makes you think of drowsy, shadow-seeking garden cats and butterflies fecklessly fluttering over potato row and currant bush—a rural homestead sequestered and solitary where only the splashes of water rats or the quaint aquatic calls of moorhens with red nebs agape and white scuts wagging, come through the open windows to disturb the afternoon silences of whitewashed chambers that, faintly smelling of goose-feather bolsters and patchwork quilts, are as cool as cider cellars.

> Carter for Mr Manley,
> He worked at Willum's Mill,
> And up by barton and down by mead
> He sang to the maidens upon his reed.
> 'Apples be ripe,' he sang to them,
> 'And nuts be brown,' they answered him.

Yet even in this island of dutiful dairy work deep surrounded by pastures blessed with the very peace of Paradise I can remember there happening once a most pitiful tragedy. The miller, a man in a small way of business whose thumbs were never golden, had two little children, his heart's delight, who, unwatched for a moment, strayed out of the house to be drowned in the millpond, so treacherously overgrown was it with willowherb, loosestrife and close-clustering meadowsweet.

Wulham's Mill! In June no fields in all England are as retired as those that surround this dreaming domicile amid the rich, corncrake-calling cow-leas of South Somerset. Over each opulent acre there hangs a peculiar glamour. At midsummer all the lanes are dry, and from end to end their hedges are garlanded with honeysuckle and dog-roses as for a festival. It is then that the deep damp ditches rustle at night with the pressing thorny shoulders of hedgehogs resolutely adventuring to drink lukewarm milk from the dripping udders of the midnight cattle, which, with many a deep exhalation from their warm, weighty carnal beings, like monuments of recumbent piety, await the coming of the sacred dawn.

It is during those sultry solstice weeks that the shadows of the hedgerow timber, of the tall shrouded elms, become more and more bewitched, moving across the buttercup grass at so listless a rate that a man leaning against one of those village field gates at noon might imagine them to be at an absolute pause—gigantic dial-hand shadows, umbrageous, clumsy and obstinate—resolved perhaps to register only those more enraptured hours when men and women are at liberty 'to fleet the time carelessly as they did in the golden world'.

Two Country Writers

Not long ago, in his great old age, Thomas Hardy made a protest against blood sports. He saw clearly that such pastimes are in their essence barbarous. The old man possessed the dangerous vision of greatness, the dangerous vision of a poet not content with any half-way beauty. All supreme artists menace the manners and preconceptions of society. The prevailing ideas, the prevailing codes of behaviour accepted by conventional persons are built up on cleverly devised systems of false thinking, by means of which such 'extraverts' seek to reconcile their lives to the rude, shocking and humanly illogical facts that lurk below existence.

If I were to offer a criticism of Henry Williamson's work, for instance—in many ways so admirable—I would say that it lacked the detached, imaginative insight, deep and philosophic, which was the natural heritage of those two great nature writers, Thomas Hardy and W. H. Hudson, and which to a lesser degree is to be found in the short animal stories of Liam O'Flaherty. Henry Williamson is a capital writer; for pages together, his style will be exceptional, but there is a weakness in him. He accepts the popular view, and the popular view is seldom the correct one. The prose of a truly great writer flashes about one's head like lightning and reveals a reality below the surface, giving a new confidence to the footfalls of wayfarers on the great turnpike highroad.

But when so much has been granted we can give him complete praise. He developed his power of observation to a very high degree. His eye is clear and his hearing acute, and he describes the visible and audible manifestations of woodland life with an intimacy that constantly takes one by surprise. The senses of the otters he so loves in *Tarka the Otter*, could hardly be more alert:

> With ears and eyes of poachers;
> Deep-earthed ones
> Turned hunters

He misses nothing. We see his 'little water wanderer' curled up in its hiding place 'twitching in sleep'. We are given a glimpse of the shy creature as it swims by moonlight in deep water 'hidden except for his nose, which pushed a ream on the surface placid in the windless night'. He has an extraordinary power of evoking a scene through the method of intimate realism. The mother of Tarka brings her prey to the river bank. She devours the fish there. 'She ate to the tail, which was left on a wad of drying mud cast from a hoof'. In the mere mention of that wad of mud 'cast from a hoof' he shows the secret of his power. Williamson again and again conjures with such strokes. An owl settles on a tree above where the otter is resting, and it hears 'the scratch of its talons as they gripped the bark'. A heron rises from its fishing pool and he causes us to see the bird at close quarters, 'with his long, thin, green toes scratching the water'. We are there on the spot. We experience it all. No sound is permitted to escape us. We mark even 'the rustling clicks of dragonflies' wings over the sun-plashy ripples'.

All would be well if the writer did not destroy our illusion by too great a faithfulness to his own method. It is too much when he includes his wealthy sporting friends in his pictures of nature! We lose faith and see him as the writer of fanciful animal stories and nothing more. He does not seem to recognise his companions for what they are and it is impossible for us to feel any enthusiasm for their brutalities. We are informed of the practice of dislodging hunted otters from their earths with acetylene gas and are made to hear the 'noises of motor cars moving slowly along the hard-rutted trackways'. The wretched little animal tries to escape downstream only to find his way barred by a living wall of 'sportsmen' standing in the water 'stocking'd leg pressed to stocking'd leg'.

The truth is, Henry Williamson can do excellently well within his limitations, but these limitations seldom allow his imagination to adventure beyond the park walls of those great West Country land-owners whose point of view he reflects. His books all give expression to the inarticulate interest these 'honest gentry' have always had in nature, these gentry who have inherited sufficient wealth to spend healthy, animal lives hunting in the open fields and fortifying their minds against the disturbing influence of intelligent reflection.

*

In the case of W. H. Hudson, appreciation of his works was a recognition that came late in the author's life. For long years he had written with little or no encouragement, and then, all at once, the clouds of obscurity lifted. The message he had to give was welcomed by an innumerable company, who, it would almost seem, had been waiting to have their thoughts and their tastes expressed and inter-preted. Contemporary men of letters vied with each other in praising the artistry of this writer who of all others is most natural and artless.

Joseph Conrad once said that Hudson 'was a product of nature', and a fine penetration was contained in this simple phrase, a penetration that goes far to explain why a generation satiated perhaps with 'fine writing' should have turned with such enthusiasm to these unaffected and direct books. For Hudson's style is as sound and honest and salubrious as is the soil of the English countryside. There is no taint of the lamp about it; less so, perhaps, than in any other English writer of equal merit. The ink of these sheets has been dried by the sun, and the pages of these books have been ruffled and turned by the wind; a thousand 'nimble emanations' rise from them—the sweet perfume of cowslip fields on the banks of the River Parrett, the pungent odour of water mint or yarrow, and the divine incense that rises out of the earth in country places where healthy men and healthy animals are gathered together.

Hudson did not require an elaborate style to produce his effects. His powers of observation and his singular memory were so certain that he was able to recreate the moods of nature by hints and whispers given to him by herself. He just put down what he saw, and heard, and felt, and tasted, and the miracle was achieved. The ingredients of the cauldron of his Celtic magic are made up of everyday simples. He believed, and I think wisely, that no art can be really great that does not spring directly out of life, out of the earth. It must manifest itself with the unconscious push and growth that a skunk cabbage displays when in springtime it first thrusts its purple, mottled, primal horns out of the swamps. To read Hudson is like living again our happiest days spent in the country. Hedge-stick in hand he rambles from horizon to horizon, and now there is wind and rain in our faces, and now the round sun is tanning our foreheads and necks with its golden light.

I like to think that his unsophisticated method of writing was derived from his New England mother. It always has seemed to me that it has upon it something of the chastity, the freshness, that we associate with the farmhouses of Maine, with their well-proportioned porches, their tidy gardens and their neatly designed well-sweeps. There is no nonsense about the unspoilt manners of New England people. They are proud and reserved, and at the same time under-standing. Hudson was all this, but there was also in him an Irish inheritance. I think if you superimpose the errant, poetic tempera-ment of the Irish on the well-ordered, deep-feeling, matter-of-fact culture of the old-fashioned inhabitants of Maine you will get as near as it is possible to get to the understanding of Hudson's peculiar gift to English literature. There are, of course, other influences to be reckoned with, especially the fact that he was born and brought up in the Argentine surrounded by 'cows and sky', 'vacas y cielo', to use the gaucho expression.

The pampas left its mark upon him, and the memories of the savage men he had talked with, of the strange birds and animals he had seen, and of the vast horizon of green and blue, accentuated, by sharp contrast, his already romantic attitude toward the English country-side. Sensitive, and aware of every mood of nature as is a wild creature, he received from the great earth-mother the secret law of the land he loved so dearly. Although he did not believe in theological dogmas, Hudson was an essentially religious man. A tree, a blade of grass, anything that was wild and natural, gave him his inspiration. Purged of personal vanity and egotism, he had the uncommon power of getting out of himself 'into nature'.

It was not only to nature that Hudson was accustomed to turn for sustenance. It is evident to anyone who reads his books carefully that he knew well the enchantment, the glamour, that is the enviable heritage of all beautiful women. His references to them are most winning. He writes as tenderly of them as he does of flowers.

It is indeed terrible to think that this passionate lover of nature was caged up in London for so many years in abject poverty, living for one week, as he confessed to Mr Morley Roberts, 'on a tin of cocoa and milk'. But as Hudson himself observed, roses and lovely creepers grew out of walls built of the skulls of cattle slaughtered with abominable cruelty in the shambles of Buenos Aires. For who knows in life's vast extravagance where and by what means beauty will come to burgeon?

Christmas in Dorset

During the morning of the first Christmas that was spent by me in Africa I remember watching from the verandah of my mud hut the swallows that were darting to and fro over the broad striped backs of a herd of grazing zebra. The sight made me homesick, not only because the African landscape seemed so removed from anything I could associate with the Christmasses of my childhood but also because I knew these little swift-winged birds would themselves in four months be flying back to Europe, as likely as not to England and possibly even to Dorset.

Christmas is the feast above all feasts to remind us of our childhood and of the home of our birthplace:

> O wild-raving winds! If you ever do roar
> By the house and the elms from where I've a-come,
> Breathe up at the window, or call at the door
> And tell you've a-found me a-thinking of home.

It is it seems necessary to be a banished man before it is possible to appreciate properly the reward of spending a Christmas at home. Whenever I have been in foreign lands at this time of year, the downs and woods and rivers and sea beaches of Dorset have always been present in my mind, as it were, under a glamour.

I have but to think of Dorchester on Christmas Eve, and I am overwhelmed with nostalgia. How blithe, how jocund the old town can look on the afternoon of Christmas Eve, with the streets crowded with people come in from neighbouring villages, their careful purses full of white-money for Christmas shopping. As I write I can see the familiar faces I know, and even the country people I do not know wear all of them in my mind's eye natural faces, faces of the kind I have been used to look upon from my childhood, so strong and recurrent are the racial types of this ancient corner of the West Country.

I can see the fish-wife with smiling red face, standing by her barrow outside The Antelope, wrapping up her herrings—herrings fat as butter—caught the night before in Weymouth Bay, herrings that lie in heaps before her like bars of silver bullion from El Dorado! I can see a squire emerge from the porch of The King's Arms, good-humoured, well-constituted, his face glowing like the apple we used to call Taunton Blacks, and with half an intention in his mind to step across the street for a case of his favourite port out of the cool cellar of Mr Hodges' honourable and ancient shop. I can see a gypsy-lad from Culliford Tree, with his large horsy-looking cap tilted awry on his free head because of its seasonable burden of holly and mistletoe. I can see the cottage woman dutifully intent upon fulfilling her missions with her little daughter anxiously watching the baby's perambulator—a darling of innocent wonder in the vigorous hurly-burly of the narrow streets.

The thought of Weymouth gives me the same feeling of homesickness. How deserted an appearance the beautiful crescent beach can present on the afternoon of Christmas Eve! Five months ago holiday visitors were crowded here in their white frocks as close as gulls; now all is abandoned and unfestive, with perhaps a single school boy, red and black cap on his young head, idly throwing pebbles for diversion of a barking dog rushing boisterously over the wide flat levels of sand, where unlooked-for, autumn-storm cowrie shells lie in all their inconspicuous beauty. In and out of the shops the people go with parcels under their arms, already anticipating the hour when they will be back at home again with the tea things on the table. How romantic the old harbour can appear, with lights coming out one by one, and boatmen chattering together before entering some snug tavern interior familiar to them for half a century; looking out, perhaps, towards White Nose and predicting snow or fumbling for a tin of tobacco in a pocket under a blue jersey—a pocket filled with string and fishing tackle and a red cotton handkerchief silvered over with fish scales wiped off in the hour of the dawn from hands rendered hard as horn by the hauling of ropes in every ocean of the round world.

How merry and mellow Christmas can still be in Dorset! Perhaps the spirit of it is best of all maintained in the more out of the way districts, in cottages standing apart in lonely byways on the Toller Down, in old mossy mills in the valley of the Stour, where little children crawl to the ends of their beds after their woollen Santa Claus stockings, at a time when all is still dark in the room and there is no sound except the monotonous music of the swirling brown waters of the river flowing on and on past Stalbridge meadows, past Blandford back gardens, down to a wintry sea of crying gulls and deserted beaches.

In scores of villages in the Blackmore Vale the season is celebrated in the traditional way. The tables of the homesteads are well-loaded and the rooms thick decorated with leaves as a forest, with many a kiss stolen and given under the mistletoe.

Thomas Hardy for all his obdurate scepticism as a poet, could never rid his mind of the old rumour of the cattle kneeling in prayer at the midnight hour. Much the same notion was entertained by William Shakespeare, who believed that the farm cocks continued to crow all through the small hours of Christmas morning to frighten away uneasy ghosts who on this evening are sometimes privileged, it has been thought, to wander beyond churchyard walls into the land of the living:

> Some say, that ever 'gainst that season comes
> Wherein our Saviour's birth is celebrated
> The bird of dawning singeth all night long;
> And then, they say, no spirit dare stir abroad:
> The nights are wholesome ...

It is interesting to try to choose among the old Christmas carols the ones that are most suitable to Dorset. It is true that all the Nativity ballads can seem fitting enough if you happen to be abroad upon the downs where sheep have been hurdled into folds under the stars!

To my mind, however, 'A Lyke-Wake Dirge' is singularly appropriate, especially when it is remembered that the 'whinnes' mentioned in the fourth verse to be used as a punishment for the sinner, are nothing else than our homely gorse bushes which are so characteristic a feature of the chalk downs from Lyme Regis to Studland. The old poem is addressed to a corpse lying beneath its shroud:

> If ever thou gavest hosen or shoon,
>   Every nighte and alle,
> Sit thee down and put them on,
>   And Christe receive thy soule
>
> If hosen and shoon thou ne'er gav'st nane
>   Every nighte and alle
> The whinnes shall prick thee to the bare bane
>   And Christe receive thy soule.

But perhaps even more suggestive of Dorset, with its silver sea coast of proud lonely headlands and dizzy far-stretching undulating cliffs, is the ballad that begins:

> I saw three ships come sailing in
>   On Christmas day, on Christmas Day,
> I saw three ships come sailing in,
>   On Christmas Day in the morning.
>
> And what was in those ships all three
>   On Christmas Day, on Christmas Day?
> And what was in those ships all three,
>   On Christmas Day in the morning?
>
> Our Saviour Christ and his ladye,
>   On Christmas Day, on Christmas Day,
> Our Saviour Christ and his ladye
>   On Christmas Day in the morning.

True Happiness

The fellow who answered the question 'Is life worth living?' with the words, 'it depends upon the liver,' uttered with his jest but a half-truth, for though there can be little doubt that a sound liver inclines us to a condition of good cheer, yet it is also a fact that a healthy body in no way renders a happy life inevitable.

People often mock at those of us who steadfastly believe in the possibility of human happiness, and true it is that there exist upon earth innumerable accidents that can render these fortunate moods difficult to come by. To begin with, we always have with us what Wordsworth named 'natural sorrows', that is to say, all those frustrations and bereavements having to do with love and death that are inseparable from our lot as human beings. Then, following close upon the heels of such yearnings and desolations, come the countless untoward circumstances brought into existence by our own wilfulness, by our own lack of foresight, and by our own folly.

Obviously the problem is a deep and confused one, and it would be easy enough to show that even a complete realisation of the triple

Christmas benediction—health, wealth and prosperity—would not make the coveted state of happiness absolutely sure. A man who has been conspicuously unsuccessful in life's scramble is often not only a more trusty companion than his vaulting, go-getting rival could ever be, but also a more frolicsome one.

The fact is, happiness is an imponderable and mysterious essence. It is not a ginger-bread to be bought with a silver sixpence at the first fair, nor can it be summoned to the knee at the first whistle like a pet basket-poodle, nor can it be counterfeited. When least deserved and least expected, there it is with us like a little girl who comes suddenly through a garden gate with meadow flowers in her hands.

It is useful, however, to clarify our understanding of the conditions 'generally necessary' for the spontaneous generation of the miracle. To be blessed with a sanguine temperament is of more consequence than anything else. Born in August, say all! But unluckily, this matter of possessing a happy temperament is beyond the province of man's direction and many a mother marvels to herself over the difference of character displayed by children brought up in the same house—this one sad and sensitive, and this one sane and sunny.

The chief mainstays of mortal felicity without doubt are love, health and work that is interesting, though even these fostering conditions cannot be considered as absolutely essential to the beatific state. I have often met with tramps and beggars, as idle as summer clouds, who yet have provided better company through their merry humour than those who, dazed and dazzled by the twinkling of golden spoons, sit fat by the fire.

Of the lesser obstacles to happiness I would most surely name ambition. Shakespeare was well aware of the danger of allowing too much scope to this form of egoism. Especially in its more petty manifestations is it able to do incalculable mischief to a free enjoyment of a life. How many foolish men and women, in Mayfair and in the side streets of every provincial town, impoverish and embitter their days by an over-indulgence of social aspirations, so that for the sake of a succession of frivolous triumphs they suffer their very hearts to be eaten out by envy, hatred and malice, even to the edge of the grave which levels in so stern and effectual a manner every human vanity. 'All's alike at the latter day, a bag of gold and a whisp of hay'.

We often hear it said that a man's happiness depends upon the strength of his religious faith. Unless we use the word 'religious' in a very broad sense I do not believe this is true. He that keeps close to Nature does not go far out of the way. First and foremost happiness has to do with loving and being loved. A silver key can open an iron lock. It has also to do with the pastimes and securities of the home, with the voices and footsteps of children, with food and drink partaken at a familiar table. It may however be heralded in a hundred indirect ways. By the distant sound of a flute or fiddle on a summer evening, by a bird at a winter window, by a sunset seen suddenly over sloping roof-tops at the end of a passage, or by the spiritual peace that accompanies gardening, even though the flowers we care for may be growing in a plot no wider than a window-sill box or the wire fern-rack of a back parlour.

Happiness depends also upon a person's having been able in his or her life to exercise and develop private and particular talents to their utmost capacity. Most certainly it does not depend upon politics. 'There are no public worries, only private worries,' said Dr Johnson. Man is not naturally vicious. Self-indulgent and lazy he may be, but his fundamental disposition is closer to that of a much-enduring ass than to that of a wall-eyed mule whose heels are over his ears.

The distractions of the present epoch result from the fact that the claims of the social contract are now so complicated and so exacting that too little room is allowed for the proper and legitimate flourishing of the life of the individual. An ox when loose licks himself with pleasure. Instead of a man having a trade of his own to excel in, or a parcel of land of his own to cultivate, he is clapped into a factory to sweat at some meaningless task-work, or at best sits perched like a monkey upon an office stool from twilight to twilight—as merry as an ape with a clog at his heel. He is in luck if he is allowed to play a game of darts at the corner pub in the evening, for even the moments of his free hours are being regimented and standardised out of all reason.

Yet even in these broken times of transition, before the greatest happiness of the greatest number of free people is recognised as the only legitimate purpose of government, it is possible for a wise man to find content. The best fish swim nearest to the bottom. Let those who like to jump after success jump and jump again; let the ambitious play at their leapfrog till death catch them by the breech. True happiness is seldom to be found in the outward stir of life. It comes to those whose creature needs are properly cared for and whose values are simple and centred in the homely and natural interests of human life.

NOTES

1   **Green Corners of Dorset.**   First published in the *Adelphi* XVI, n.s No.3 (December 1939). I have edited somewhat, correcting misprints and omitting two short paragraphs which referred to the current war. The original printing also came with an epigraph, 'O sweet Fancy! Let her loose!' (the MS title of the piece). The first quoted passage is from Claudio's speech in *Measure for Measure*, Act III, sc.1.

2   **The Parson of Broadwindsor.**   First published as 'Thomas Fuller—The Cavalier Parson of Broadwindsor' in the *Dorset Daily Echo*, 21 September 1935. I have made some changes of paragraphing and minor corrections. The use of the word 'dorser' in the second paragraph would seem to be incorrect. Llewelyn might have imagined a 'dorser' was a carrier of panniers rather than the pannier itself, or he might have meant 'dosser', one who travels around. 'John Dorys' were mackerel.

3   **Gypsies at Weymouth Market.**   First published as 'Gypsies Come to Weymouth Market House' in the *Dorset Daily Echo*, 28 October 1933. I have corrected some misprints and changed some of the paragraphing.

4   **Betsy Cooper.**   This is an early memory of Nancy Cooper (d.*c*.1902), the Montacute vagabond, and her daughter Betsy, whom Llewelyn later wrote about more fully in the essay 'Nancy Cooper' published in *Somerset Essays* (1937), and in 'Montacute House' in the same book. Llewelyn Powys tried his hand at several stories based upon the figure of the old woman; this one was probably written in *c*.1915–19, and conflates the two figures, hence I have tried to disentangle them. The text is taken from Alyse Gregory's 1950s typescript of a MS draft (Sims II:51) at the HRHRC, Austin, Texas, which she called 'Nancy Cooper'.

5   **The Swannery Bell at Abbotsbury.**   This was written in 1935 and first published in the *Dorset Daily Echo*, 19 September 1936.

6   **Dorset Ovens.** Taken from a prepared MS at the HRHRC, Austin, Texas. (Sims IV:21)

7   **Lodmoor.**   First published in the *Fig Tree: A Douglas Social Credit Quarterly Review* No.3 (December 1936); republished in *The Powys Journal* II (1992). The couplet is from Chaucer's *The Knight's Tale*.

8   **The Wordsworths in Dorset.** First published in the *Dorset Daily Echo*, 1 August 1936, and later brought out in a slightly expanded version as a limited edition by Covent Garden Press in conjunction with INCA Books, 1972, under the editorship of Malcolm Elwin (who treated it as unpublished). Powys probably

wrote it at the same time as he was reviewing Ernest de Selincourt's edition of *The Early Letters of William and Dorothy Wordsworth* (1935), published under the title 'The Wordsworths' in the *American Mercury* (April 1936). The quotation is from Burns's 'On Seeing a Wounded Hare Limp by Me'. Wordsworth's word 'vectigal' seems to be an invention of his, meaning direction or course, whereas Llewelyn's word 'tod' is Spenserean, meaning a bush. The death of Wordsworth's brother John in the wreck of the *Abergavenny* was the subject of Llewelyn's essay 'A Famous Wreck' which was collected into *Somerset Essays* (1937).

9   **Birds of a Winter Garden.**   First published in a shorter version in the *Spectator* CLIV (8 February 1935). I have followed a typescript by Alyse Gregory made, it would seem, later and tidied up by her. However this also preserves some original touches such as 'pink, pink' for the sound of the chaffinch rather than the printed version's 'peep, peep'. The former is undoubtedly more accurate. The printed version corrected Llewelyn's quotation from Bewick, and that I have incorporated.

10   **The Chesil Beach.**   First published in a shorter version in *Time and Tide* (12 August 1939). I have followed a typescript by Alyse Gregory, with some editing and the omission of one paragraph about sea-rovers in Elizabethan times. 'Deadman's Bay' was Hardy's name for Weymouth Bay in *The Well-Beloved*.

11   **One of a Thousand.**   First published in the *Weymouth and District Hospital Carnival Programme* for 1931. This is the earliest of the published essays reproduced here and reflects Llewelyn's more fatalistic attitude which is present in the collection *Earth Memories*, mostly essays of the 1920s although published in 1934. I have made a few small alterations and have kept the spelling of 'White Nore' as it is in the original, although Llewelyn by this time was calling the headland 'White Nose' in accordance with Hardy's view (see following essay). The editor of the magazine no doubt changed it back, since 'White Nore' is more authentic. The original was illustrated with a drawing of a razor-bill.

12   **A Downland Burden.**   This was written in 1936. The draft appears in a notebook marked 26a (Sims II:27) at the HRHRC, Austin, Texas, which also has Alyse Gregory's typescript of the 1950s. It is headed by a quote which I have omitted: 'Red in the morning is the shepherd's warning'. The account of Llewelyn's walk with the pack of herrings in the early morning from Jordan Hill to East Chaldon is told in a fabricated diary of 1919 (see 'An Exile's Return', *The Powys Journal* X, 2000, pp.29-41).

13   **Recollections of Thomas Hardy.**   This is the most complete version of an essay originally published in *The Virginia Quarterly Review* XV, No.3 (July 1939). This longer version was published by Kenneth Hopkins in his *Selection from the Writings of Llewelyn Powys* (1952). Another truncated version was published by Toucan Press in 1969. The first quoted poem is John Cowper Powys's 'To Thomas Hardy' published in his *Odes and Other Poems* of 1896. This dates the first visit of

Hardy to Montacute when Llewelyn was 12 or 13 years old. Hopkins's version cited three verses of Hardy's poem 'Afterwards'; I have quoted only the first.

14 **Hedgehogs.** First published as 'Thrice and Once the Hedgehog Whined' in the *Dorset Daily Echo*, 14 November 1936. I have corrected some hyphenation and omitted the quote—misquoted—from *Macbeth* Act IV, sc.1, which heads the piece.

15 **Chainey Bottom.** First published as 'Llewelyn Powys Picks up Flints' in the *Dorset Daily Echo*, 30 March 1935. I have returned the spelling of 'Chainey' as Llewelyn used it, although the newspaper, which was not too clear in its understanding of the piece, had 'Chainy' throughout. Llewelyn's brother, A. R. Powys, who helped supervise the small excavation at Chainey Bottom in 1930, wrote a report, now at the Dorset County Museum, headed 'Notes on a Flint-filled Hollow in Chainey Bottom between Bat's Head and Swyre Head'. L. F. Salzman was the celebrated medieval historian, renting one of the coastguard cottages at the time. A further version of the same material was published as 'A Dorset Bronze Age Valley' in 1935 (and collected into *Somerset Essays*, 1937).

16 **Worked Flints.** This is taken from a rough typescript copy by Alyse Gregory of some fragments on the prehistory of the downs and the collecting of worked flints which Llewelyn wrote up in a notebook of c.1932 now at the HRHRC, Austin, Texas (Sims II:70). I have refashioned the piece by amalgamating parts of two separate fragments.

17 **Guests of Grace.** First published in the *Countryman* (April 1935). I have edited it somewhat in accordance with proofed notes by Alyse Gregory. I have also substituted the word 'sun' for 'Ra-Heracti' at the end of the second paragraph, as making the sense clearer. Llewelyn used the term 'Aryan' for what would now be referred to by etymologists as 'Indo-European'. His derivation of 'bee' is suspect, and may come from Skeat, whose *Concise Etymological Dictionary of the English Language* Llewelyn owned—and used—in its 1927 edition. The flint cottage was Chydyok on the downs south of Chaldon Herring, Dorset.

18 **Robert Herrick.** First published in the *Saturday Review of Literature*, 8 February 1936. I have converted American spellings to English and corrected Llewelyn's quotations from Herrick. I have also omitted two passages, one in the fourth paragraph about men's attitude to women, and the other at the end of the essay where Llewelyn includes some random quotes summarising Herrick's philosophy. The passages from Herrick are as follows: from *Hesperides* (1662): the final couplet; 'Upon a Bleare-Ey'd Woman', No.222; 'The Captiv'd Bee; Or, The Little Filcher', No.182; 'Love Perfumes All Parts', No.155; 'Upon the Nipples of Julia's Breast', No.441; 'Upon Julia's Sweat', No.720; 'To Diademe', No.404; 'To Mistresse Dorothy Parsons', No.501; 'On Tomasin Parsons', No.980; from *Noble Numbers* (166), 'To His Angrie God', No.56; 'A Thanksgiving to God for His House', No.47 (of which the third stanza is transposed from earlier in the poem).

19   **South Somerset Names.**   First published as 'South Somerset Memories' in the *Western Gazette*, 4 August 1939. The original title of the essay seems to have been 'Long Lasting Local Names in the Yeovil District'. I have omitted the epigraph from *The Book of Wisdom* ('The Wisdom of Solomon' in the *Apocrypha*): 'For our time is a very shadow that passeth away'. Llewelyn made use of Eilert Ekwall's *Oxford Dictionary of English Place-Names* (first published in 1936), some of the understandings of which have since been updated and improved upon by Margaret Gelling and others. The Blackmore Vale was the local hunt.

20   **Hedgecock Memories.**   First published as 'Hedgecock' in the *West Country Magazine* No.2 (August 1946); republished in the *The Powys Journal* V (1995). I have amended some of the hyphenation. Dr Hensleigh Walter was an amateur local historian resident in Norton-sub-Hamdon, and East Stoke Lodge neighboured Montacute Vicarage in the parish of Stoke.

21   **Montacute Mills.**   First published as 'Delights of Somerset Mills' in *Country Life* LXXXIX, 24 May 1941, where it appeared accompanied by two pictures of Montacute Mill and Welham's Mill. William Allingham (1824–1889) was a popular poet of the Victorian period, and his poem 'The Fairies'—much liked by Llewelyn in childhood—appeared in Quiller-Couch's *Oxford Book of English Verse*, owned by Llewelyn. The fourth quotation is from John Cowper Powys's poem 'The Recruit', *Wolf's-Bane* (1916). The Mill there is called 'Willum's', and I have therefore amended Llewelyn's reference.

22   **Two Country Writers.**   This essay, with my own title, incorporates two pieces Llewelyn Powys wrote towards the end of the twenties, one a review of Henry Williamson's *Tarka the Otter* which appeared in the *New York Herald Tribune*, 4 March 1928, and the other 'An Appreciation of W. H. Hudson', from the *Mobile Press*, 18 January 1930. I have adapted the articles somewhat, transposing some paragraphs and shortening the Williamson review. The reference to the 'skunk cabbage' evidences the American audience.

23   **Christmas in Dorset.**   First published as 'Oh to be in Dorset—Now with Christmas Here' in the *Dorset Daily Echo*, 24 December 1937. The first quotation is from William Barnes's 'Jenny Out Vrom Hwome', rendered into standard English (by Llewelyn). The second quotation is from *Hamlet* Act I, sc.l, 157 (Marcellus's speech before the appearance of the ghost). I have amended it somewhat. The 'Lyke Wake Dirge' was a traditional Cleveland ballad.

24   **True Happiness.**   First published as 'True Happiness Comes to Those Whose Values Are Simple', in the *Western Mail*, 3 July 1939, where the article was severely mangled. I have omitted several aphorisms, of which this essay has more than its fair share, and altered 'frolic' to frolicsome, as being more appropriate in this context, although Llewelyn was partial to the archaic form.

THE POWYS SOCIETY

President Glen Cavaliero

The Powys Society is a registered charity, No 801332

The Powys Society was founded in 1967 to 'establish the true literary status of the Powys family through promotion of the reading and discussion of their works', in particular those of John Cowper Powys (1872–1963), Theodore Francis Powys (1875–1953), and Llewelyn Powys (1884–1939).

The Society publishes a journal and three newsletters a year, and has embarked on a publication programme. In addition it organises an annual weekend conference, occasional meetings, exhibitions, and walks in areas associated with the Powys family.

The Society is an international one, attracting scholars and non-academics from around the world, and welcomes everyone interested in learning more about this remarkable family.

**For further information
and membership enquiries
please visit The Powys Society website:**

www.powys-society.org